Take toilet paper to a new dimension and revolutionize your use of a bathroom basic!

TOILET PAPER CRAFTS
FOR HOLIDAYS AND SPECIAL OCCASIONS

~

Linda Wright

This one-of-a-kind book will teach you how to make beautiful, budget-friendly projects that will add joy and festivity to any popular celebration including birthdays, weddings, and Christmas. Step-by-step illustrated instructions are provided for 60 delightful designs along with 70 full-size copy-or-trace templates to ensure your success. Crafters of all ages and experience levels will enjoy using hand and machine stitchery, folding, and basic craft techniques to repurpose bath tissue into charming new creations.

Also by Linda Wright

TOILET PAPER ORIGAMI

Delight your Guests with Fancy Folds
and Simple Surface Embellishments

TOILET PAPER CRAFTS

FOR HOLIDAYS AND SPECIAL OCCASIONS

....

60 Papercraft, Sewing, Origami and Kanzashi Projects

LINDA WRIGHT

To MSR and JRR, with love

For more inspiration, visit www.toiletpapercrafts.com.

Become a fan of TOILET PAPER CRAFTS on Facebook!

Reprints of this book may be ordered at Amazon.com.

For information regarding quantity discounts for bulk purchases for sales promotions, premiums, or educational use, or for special editions or book excerpts created to specification, contact sales@lindaloo.com.

Edition 1.0
Printed in the United States of America

Lindaloo Enterprises
P.O. Box 90135
Santa Barbara, CA 93190
sales@lindaloo.com

ISBN: 9780980092325

Library of Congress Control Number: 2010903024

Life is like a roll of toilet paper . . .
the closer you get to the end,
the faster it goes.

Contents

INTRODUCTION

Get ready for the fun and unforgettable world of toilet paper crafts! Within these pages lies a delightful array of designs created from a simple necessity. You will find stylish projects appropriate for any holiday—and many special occasions—including birthdays, weddings, Christmas, new babies, showers, anniversaries, and graduations.

By trying any and every brand of bath tissue I could find, I learned that toilet papers all have unique properties that can be used to your advantage. Among the 2-ply products on the market, some have plies that are extremely easy to separate. This is a welcome feature for objects that require ply separation—such as pom poms or flowers. Others take a bit more effort to pull apart, and one noteworthy product does not separate at all. With layers laminated together, Cottonelle Ultra is weighty, substantial, and a favorite for designs based on kanzashi (the Japanese art of fabric folding), bows, hanging banners, and the Honeycomb Garland.

Charmin Ultra Soft is remarkable for the way it looks and behaves like fabric. It is soft, drapeable, and perfect for the Ruffled Heart Card and Rosette Brooch.

The crispness of bath tissue made from recycled paper, such as Full Circle and Bright Green, enables them to fluff beautifully when the plies are separated—and keep their shape. They hold a nice crease. And when reduced to pulp and dried, they make a strong homemade paper.

While I primarily use 2-ply toilet paper, 1-ply also has its place. Charmin Basic has a unique stretchability that makes it exceptional for crafting the Origami Rose. This same product also has a see-through property that is key to the success of hand embroidered toilet paper.

Last, but not least, the embossing is a major attraction in the use of bath tissue as a craft material. At times, this alone determines my choice of product. Some brands are quite ornamental—others more understated—and all are beautiful in their own right. I like a diamond pattern for Clown Cupcake Toppers, the simple ridges of Cottonelle for mummy costumes, and the graceful spirals of Angel Soft for a dazzling Toilet Paper Cake.

These projects were created with all age groups in mind, and many would be fun for children. From decorations and gifts, to party favors, costumes, garnishes, and greeting cards, I hope that you will enjoy making these projects as much as I enjoyed designing them. When light shines through the thin layers of a toilet paper flower, snowflake, pom pom, or garland, it is truly a beautiful sight. You will never look at toilet paper the same way again. Let's get rolling!

Why Toilet Paper?

Humorous as it sounds, toilet paper makes an ideal material for crafts. It is readily available, inexpensive, and versatile. You can cut, fold, glitter, glue, scrunch, twist, paint, or sew it. Embossed with ornamental patterns, it gives the crafter a head start on embellishment. Its strip format and perforations eliminate a lot of measuring and cutting, and save time. Its classic color, white, is refreshing and elegant, complementing and enhancing any decor. Toilet paper lends itself well to the temporary nature of special occasion decorations, yet can also be transformed into beautiful new objects that are surprisingly strong. Best of all, crafting with toilet paper is lots of fun! The very quirkiness of creating lovely items from such a supply is guaranteed to put a twinkle in your eye, and a smile on your face.

Choosing Toilet Paper for Crafts

All toilet paper is not created equal. Some is thick, some thin, some soft, and some crisp. The brand you prefer for personal use may not be the one best suited for crafts, so how do you choose? For starters, refer to the Resources section at the back of this book. Here you will see what I used for my samples. As you become more experienced in working with different products, the paper selection process becomes easier. Let's look at the considerations.

Ply

Ply refers to layers of paper. A 1-ply toilet paper consists of 1 layer, 2-ply has 2 layers, and so on. Two-ply is the most common, and the best choice for most of the projects in this book. For some designs, the plies must be separated, and there is wide variation in the ease in which plies can be pulled apart.

Fiber Content

Premium toilet papers are made from virgin wood fibers. These are the softest and thickest. Cottonelle, Charmin, and Quilted Northern fall into this category. This type of product excels for many projects. Other notable brands are those made

3

from recycled paper, such as Bright Green, Full Circle, and Marcal. Most of the bath tissues made from recycled content have a crisp hand and lots of body. They fluff up wonderfully when the plies are separated, and hold their shape well.

Embossing

The best part of selecting toilet paper is for its embossing. You will find many lovely motifs including flowers, foliage, dots, diamonds, hearts, ridges, and swirls. Choose a pattern that will complement and enhance your project.

Color

Toilet paper is predominantly white in the United States, though colors can be found. Scott's Soft Colors are 1-ply toilet papers in pastel pink, green, or blue. Angel Soft's Pretty Prints have a delicate pink and green floral pattern that is perfect for Kanzashi Flowers or Confetti Eggs. Bright colors that are popular in Europe, such as Renova's bold red, orange, lime green, fuchsia, turquoise, and black, can sometimes be found online.

Size

Though size is not a major consideration, it is good to be aware of the variations in size of toilet paper sheets, and toilet paper rolls. At-home rolls of bath tissue can be regular, double, triple, big, giant, or mega. The only time this is a factor is for building the Toilet Paper Cake—where roll size will determine the final proportion. As for the size of an individual "square", or sheet of toilet paper between perforations, this is very similar among brands. Nearly all, except Marcal, measure 4 inches between perforations. (Marcal measures $3^5/_8$ inches between perforations.) Roll widths will vary from $4^1/_4$ inches to $4^1/_2$ inches, but all will work equally well.

General Directions

1. Read through a project in its entirety before you begin. For origami and kanzashi items, look to the next photo as you fold. It will help you understand where you are going.

2. The right side of toilet paper is the side facing outward on a new roll. The underside is also called the wrong side.

3. TP will sometimes be used as an abbreviation for toilet paper.

4. A square refers to one sheet of toilet paper between perforations. Toilet paper squares are not perfectly square.

5. To fan-fold, or accordion-fold, alternate between folding the paper in front and behind the strip.

6. Use sharp scissors for cutting. It is best to have several sizes. Small scissors, such as manicure scissors or embroidery scissors, are best for intricate cuts, while larger ones excel for bigger sweeps.

7. To fold paper lengthwise, fold parallel to the lengthwise edge. The length of the paper will stay the same. To fold widthwise, fold parallel to the widthwise edge. The width of the paper will stay the same.

8, When using floral tape, stretch and pull as you wrap. This will enable the tape to stick to itself.

9. Use a ballpoint pen to trace templates onto toilet paper.

10. All templates are provided at actual size.

11. Cutting lines are depicted as solid lines. Dotted lines will refer to folding lines or stitching lines, as directed.

12. Choose a strong general-purpose thread for projects that involve stitchery.

13. Floral wire is sold in gauges: the higher the gauge, the thinner the wire. Two sizes that will meet most of your needs are 18 gauge and 22 gauge. Available plain or wrapped in cloth, cloth-wrapped wire is easier to use due to its ability to help grip the toilet paper.

14. To facilitate punching holes in toilet paper, hold it against copy paper and punch through all layers.

15. Krylon silver glitter spray will give any of these projects a beautiful shimmer.

16. Toilet paper can be tinted with any all-purpose spray paint.

17. Be careful when using a hot glue gun. A dab of hot glue on skin can burn, so keep a small dish of water handy.

18. Toilet paper is very flammable. Do not place these projects near an open flame.

19. Visit www.toiletpapercrafts.com and Toilet Paper Crafts on Facebook to view color photos of various projects and find fresh inspiration. Be sure to share photographs of your own bath tissue creations on the Toilet Paper Crafts fan page on Facebook for all to enjoy!

PROJECTS

FLOWERS

Learn to make beautiful flowers with two simple techniques: the Bowtie Method and the Wraparound Method. Choose a 2-ply toilet paper with a crisp texture. Bath tissues made from recycled paper are generally ideal. Add delicate layers of spray paint or glitter spray to finished flowers for stunning results.

Supplies: 2-ply toilet paper, cloth-wrapped floral wire or pipe cleaners, scissors, floral tape, ballpoint pen, Krylon silver glitter spray (optional), spray paint (optional)

Instructions

DAHLIA, PEONIE & CARNATION

These flowers are made using the Bowtie Method—a procedure based on a common bow-making technique. Change the shape of your cut in Step 5 to make 3 different flowers.

1. Tear off a 4-square strip of toilet paper, and fan-fold it along the perforations to make a stack **(a)**.

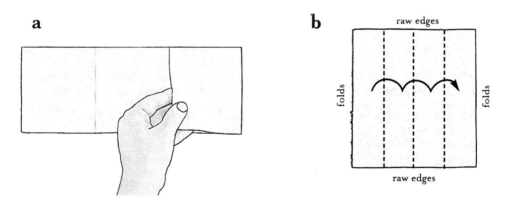

2. Fan-fold the stack into 4 equal sections **(b)**. Each fold should be about 1 inch wide.

TOP TIP

Bath tissue made from recycled paper is ideal for flower making.

3. Fold and unfold the stack in half widthwise to mark the center with a crease **(c)**.

c   **d**

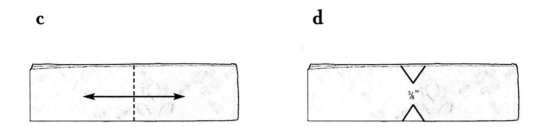

4. Cut notches at the center, leaving ⅜ inch of paper intact **(d)**.

5. Cut the ends of your paper stack into 1 point for a Dahlia, several points for a Carnation, or a curve for a Peonie. Use the templates below for cutting guides. Cut only on the solid lines, leaving the toilet paper uncut along each side.

Copy-or-Trace Templates

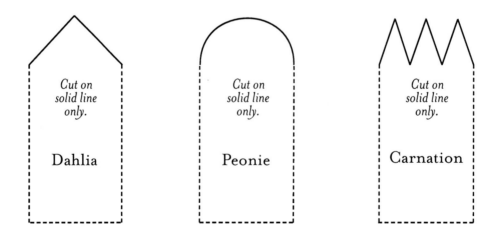

Cut on
solid line
only.

Dahlia

Cut on
solid line
only.

Peonie

Cut on
solid line
only.

Carnation

6. Hold your stack horizontally, folded edges facing up, and wrap wire or a pipe cleaner around the center. Twist the wire at the underside to secure (e).

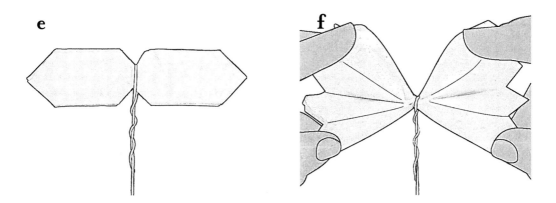

7. Unfold the fans. Start at the top layer to gently separate the layers, including the plies, and fluff the flower into shape (f).

8. Cover the stem wire with floral tape, if desired. Work from the top to the bottom, and stretch the tape as you wrap (g). Tint the finished flower with spray paint, or add shimmer with glitter spray, if desired.

TOP TIP

Floral tape is available in green, brown or white. Stretch it while you wrap to activate the adhesive.

DAISY, GARDENIA, COSMO & POINSETTIA

These flowers are made using the Wraparound Method—where a strip of petals is rolled around a center piece. Change the shape of your cut in Step 5 to get 4 different flowers.

1. Center piece: Tear off 2 squares of toilet paper. Crumple 1 of the squares into a tight ball around the top of your stem wire or pipe cleaner **(a)**.

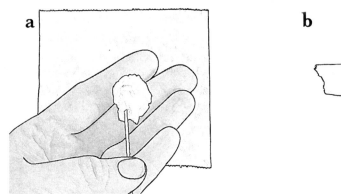
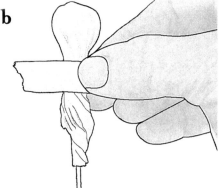

2. Drape the 2nd square over the ball. Twist the raw edges around the stem, and secure it with floral tape **(b)**.

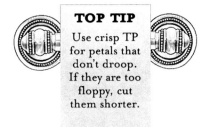

TOP TIP
Use crisp TP for petals that don't droop. If they are too floppy, cut them shorter.

3. Tear off a 4-square strip of toilet paper, and fan-fold it along the perforations to make a stack (c).

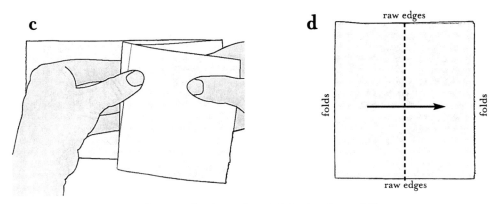

4. Fold the stack in half—parallel to the folded edges (d).

5. Cut a petal shape using a template from page 14 or 15. Be sure to cut only on the solid line (e). Unfold.

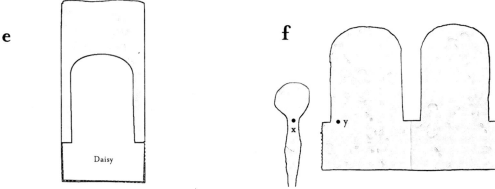

6. Place the strip with the base of the first petal at the base of the center piece, matching up points x and y (f). Wrap the strip around the center piece—pleating the paper as you wrap—so that the petals meet and fullness is created.

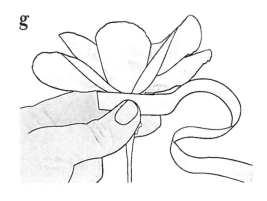

7. Secure the bottom of the flower with floral tape, and continue wrapping the tape downward to cover the stem. Stretch the tape as you go (g). Tint lightly with spray paint, or add shimmer with glitter spray, if desired.

Copy-or-Trace
Templates

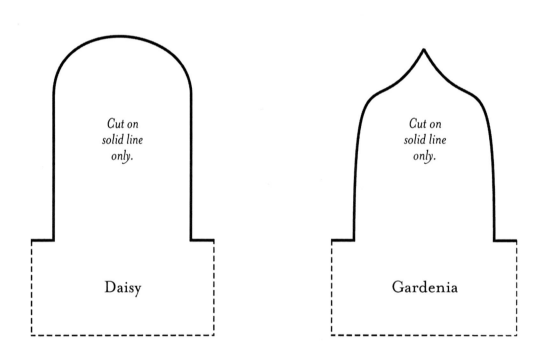

Cut on
solid line
only.

Daisy

Cut on
solid line
only.

Gardenia

Copy-or-Trace
Templates

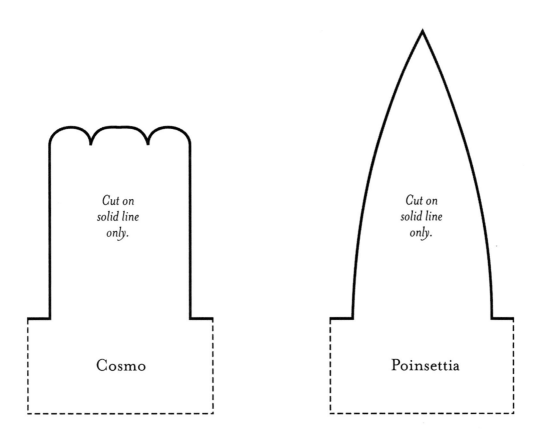

*Cut on
solid line
only.*

*Cut on
solid line
only.*

Cosmo

Poinsettia

CHRYSANTHEMUM

Mum's the word! This Wraparound style
is made with a fringed center piece.

1. Tear off a 5-square strip of toilet paper, and fold it in half lengthwise **(a)**. Fan-fold the strip on the perforations to make a stack.

a

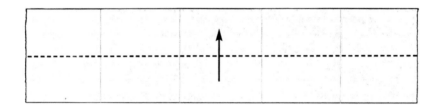

2. Cut into the raw edges—through all layers—at ³⁄₈-inch intervals, leaving ½ inch uncut at the folded edge **(b)**.

b

Raw Edges

Leave ½ inch uncut here

Folds

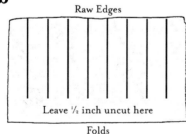

c

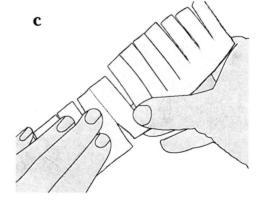

3. Gently unfold to reveal a long fringed strip. Tear 1 square off at the perforation **(c)**.

4. Center piece: Using the single square, place the tip of your floral wire or pipe cleaner at the base of the fringe **(d)**. Wrap the paper tightly around the wire, and secure it with floral tape.

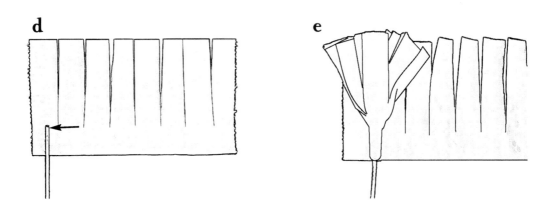

5. Place the remaining strip against the center piece **(e),** and wrap it gently around the stem. Use care not to catch any fringes in your wraps.

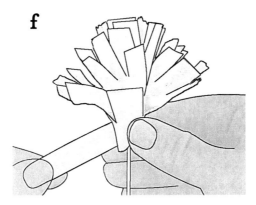

6. Secure the bottom of the flower with floral tape, and continue wrapping downward to cover the stem. Stretch the tape as you wrap **(f).**

TOP TIP
Add sparkle with glitter spray, or a colorful tint with spray paint.

ROSE

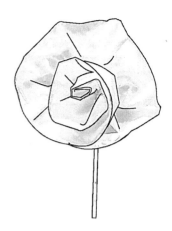

Anyone can have a green thumb with this easy flower.
Make one fold—and roll it up!

1. Tear off a 4-square strip of toilet paper, and fold it in half lengthwise **(a)**.

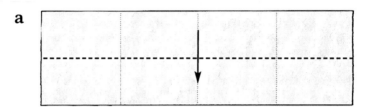

2. With the folded edge of the strip facing upward, place the stem along one end, positioning the tip of the stem halfway between the upper and lower edges **(b)**. Begin rolling the toilet paper around the stem, wrapping the first inch tightly. Continue to wrap, pleating the paper as you go.

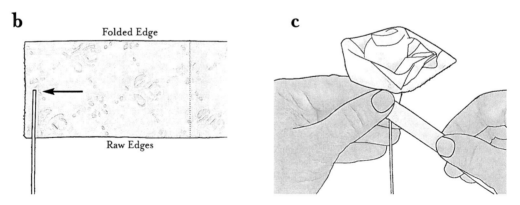

3. Secure the bottom of the flower with floral tape, and continue wrapping the tape downward to cover the stem—stretching the tape as you wrap **(c)**. Tuck the raw edge of the flower into the fold. Tint with spray paint, or add shimmer with glitter spray, if desired.

TOP TIP

Add
fragrance
to roses
with a
light spray
of perfume.

BLOSSOMS & BIRDS MOBILE

The arrival of a new baby is one of life's most special occasions—and this charming mobile would be a sweet addition to any nursery. Textural bird bodies are made from toilet paper pulp, and delicate wings from pleated squares of toilet paper. For an attractive alternative, instructions are provided for bird bodies made from paper plates.

Supplies: toilet paper, tree branch, invisible nylon thread, brown floral tape, 1/8-inch hole punch, scissors, pencil, ballpoint pen, hot glue, ridged-edge paper plates (optional)

Instructions

1. Branch: Gather a branch in a configuration that you like, and remove any leaves. Attach 2 or 3 generous lengths of thread with a Lark's Head Knot, choosing your locations so that the branch will balance. Hold all thread ends together above the branch, visualizing how you want it to hang, and adjust until the branch is nicely horizontal. Tie all threads together with an overhand knot, then tie them again in a second overhand knot, three inches above the first. Snip off loose ends.

HOW TO TIE A LARK'S HEAD KNOT

The Lark's Head Knot is tied around a support piece. In this project, the support will be the branch or the bird. First, cut a thread, and make a loop in the center. Place it under the support piece. The loop should be close to you—and the ends farther away. Next, take both ends, bring them over the support piece, and pass them through the loop. Pull the ends to make a snug knot.

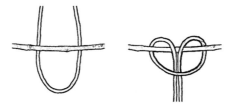

2. Bird Bodies: Make 5 pieces of homemade paper following the instructions on page 109. Using the template on page 23, trace bird bodies onto the homemade paper with a ballpoint pen, and cut them out. Cut a slit and punch 6 holes in each bird as shown on the template.

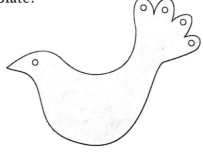

For a variation, the bird bodies can be made from paper plates. For this option, trace the bird template onto a paper plate, positioning it so that the tail feathers align with the ridges on the edge of the plate. Cut out the birds, and flatten the base of their tails a bit with your hand if the rim of the plate is very curved. Cut slits and punch holes as shown on the template.

3. Wings: Take 1 square of toilet paper and fan-fold, perpendicular to the perforated edges, in ½-inch folds **(a)**.

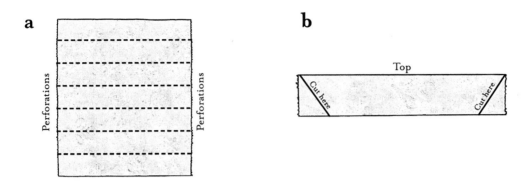

4. Make a diagonal cut across each end, as shown **(b)**.

5. Assembly: Cut 2 pieces of thread—length depending on how low you want the bird to hang. Make a loop in the center, and pass each thread through a hole on the bird body (see template). Tie with a Lark's Head Knot. Insert the wings in the slit on the bird body, centered, making sure to push the wings all the way into the punched hole. Gather all threads together above the bird, adjust until the bird is balanced horizontally, and tie with an overhand knot. To hang the bird, tie the loose thread ends over the branch, and trim the excess. Repeat steps 2-4 to make four more birds.

6. Blossoms: Follow steps c-i.

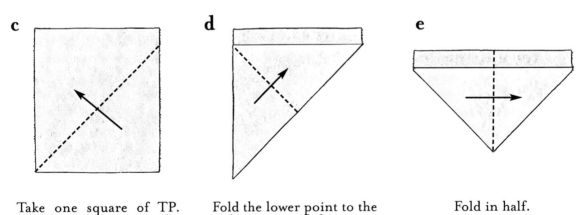

Take one square of TP. Fold the right corner to the left side, forming a triangle.

Fold the lower point to the right corner of the triangle.

Fold in half.

f

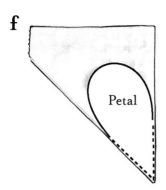

Place the petal template as shown. Trace the template onto the toilet paper with a ballpoint pen, and cut on the solid line.

g

Unfold.

h

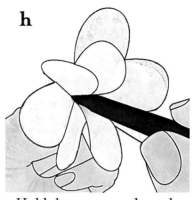

Hold the paper, and gently push into the center using the retracted tip of a ballpoint pen.

i

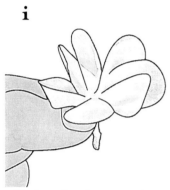

Twist the bottom into a tiny stem, and arrange the petals for a pleasing shape.

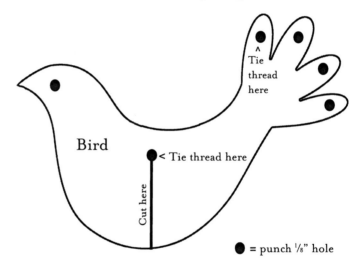

Bird

˄
Tie thread here

< Tie thread here

Cut here

⬤ = punch ⅛" hole

7. Wrap the stem with brown floral tape, and cut the stem length to ¼ inch. Repeat step 6 to make as many blossoms as desired. Attach blossoms to the branch with hot glue.

TOP TIP
Spray mobile with Krylon silver glitter spray for a sparkly finish.

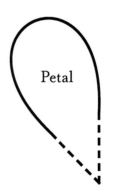

Petal

23

Pom Poms

Turn the simplest event into a party with big, beautiful Pom Poms—made with your sewing machine. Create a cluster for impact, two sizes for interest, and fasten them easily to the ceiling with mounting putty. They're cheerful, light, and lively!

Supplies: 2-ply toilet paper, sewing machine, white thread, scissors, straight pins, Krylon silver glitter spray (optional)

Instructions

LARGE POM POM
7 ½ inch diameter

1. Tear off two 6- or 7-square strips of toilet paper, and stack them on top of each other. Repeat. You should now have 2 stacks of 2 strips **(a)**.

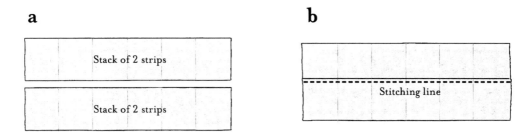

a

> Stack of 2 strips
>
> Stack of 2 strips

b

> Stitching line

2. Overlap the stacks lengthwise by ½ inch and pin in place **(b)**. Machine stitch down the center with a long stitch length, leaving long tails of thread at each end.

3. Pull the bobbin threads, and push the paper tightly to the center to gather **(c)**.

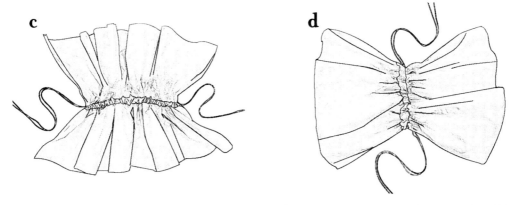

c

d

4. Tie all 4 threads together with a double knot to form a loop of ruffles **(d)**. Gently separate the paper layers—including the plies—and fluff them into shape. You will see that the loose corners of the toilet paper form points. To hang a Pom Pom with points up, tie a knot at the tail end of the threads to create a loop, and you're finished. To hang a Pom Pom with points down, wrap each set of threads to the opposite side along the stitching line, and tie in place. Knot the threads again at the tail end to create a loop for hanging. *Note: Pom Poms will stay more rounded at the top if you hang them with points facing downward.* Coat lightly with glitter spray, if desired.

SMALL POM POM
4 inch diameter

1. Tear off two 6-square strips of toilet paper, and stack them directly on top of each other. Machine stitch lengthwise down the center with a long stitch length. Leave long tails of thread at each end (a).

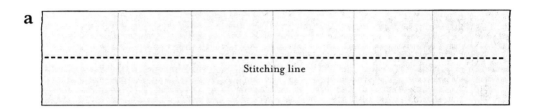

a

Stitching line

2. Pull on the bobbin threads, and push the paper tightly to the center to gather. Tie all 4 threads together with a double knot to form a loop of ruffles. Gently separate the paper layers—including the plies—and fluff them into shape. Tie a knot at the tail end of the threads to create a loop for hanging. Coat lightly with glitter spray, if desired.

TOP TIP

Hang Pom Poms from the ceiling with removable mounting putty.

Honeycomb Garland

Decorating doesn't get any easier than this! Add a festive flair to any type of party in minutes—for pennies.

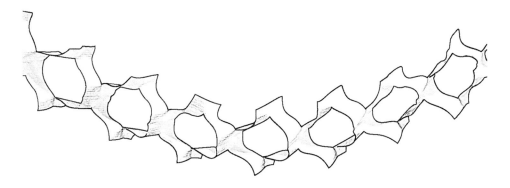

Supplies: toilet paper, scissors, ruler, ballpoint pen

Instructions

1. Fold a long strip of toilet paper in half lengthwise **(a)**.

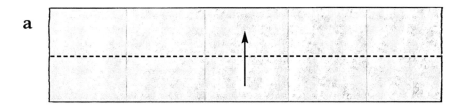

a

2. Cut into the lengthwise edges at 1-inch intervals, alternating from side to side and cutting up to ½ inch of the edge **(b)**. You can draw the cutting lines with a pen if you like, or make the cuts freehand. Unfold, and gently pull to open. For a longer garland, make more strips, and tape the pieces together.

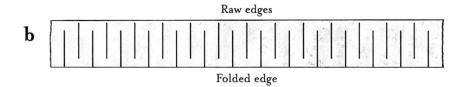

Raw edges

b

Folded edge

PETAL MASKS

In a beautiful process adapted from kanzashi, the Japanese art of fabric folding, individual squares of toilet paper are folded into simple petals, then overlapped and arranged on a base of adhesive felt. These masks feature paper eye liners trimmed with sequins, and optional handles made from branches. Not for the faint of hand, petal masks are challenging—but showstopping enough to be worth the effort.

Supplies: toilet paper, 2 pieces of white 9-by-12-inch Stick-It Felt (stiff, adhesive-backed felt), medium-weight white paper, large tweezers, white glue, ½-yard sequin trim, Scotch tape, ballpoint pen, scissors, craft knife, forked branch, hot glue, 22-gauge white floral wire (butterfly antennae only), Krylon silver glitter spray (optional), spray paint (optional), ribbon (optional)

BUTTERFLY

1. Front mask: Copy the left and right butterfly templates. Tape the sections together on the dotted lines. Trace the template onto the felt side of Stick-It Felt. Using a craft knife, cut around the perimeter, and cut out the eyes. *Be sure to cut on the inner black lines for the eyes.* Peel off the release paper.

2. Petals: Make petals from toilet paper following the instructions on pages 82 and 83, steps 1-6. Shape them as shown (**a**). Apply petals to the adhesive with tweezers. Refer to the illustration of the completed project on page 28 for placement guidelines. Start at the center (with the butterfly's body), then work outward around the perimeter of the wings, placing petals so that their tip extends slightly off the edge of the felt. Press with tweezers into the lowest folds until the petals stick. *Note: the adhesive is very sticky! Be careful not to lay your hand on it. Use a scrap of release paper to make a hand rest.* Fill in the remaining area by overlapping and staggering the petals—and continuing to work toward the center. You may need to cut some petals shorter, or shape some wider, to fill the spaces.

a

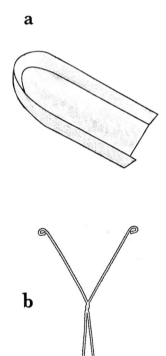

b

3. Antennae: Bend floral wire at the center into a narrow U. Twist the sides together 2 inches from the base of the U (**b**). Trim the ends to your desired length, and bend the tips into tiny loops with tweezers. Set aside.

4. Eye liners: Using the template for a guide, cut 2 eye liners from medium-weight paper. Snip as marked along the lengthwise edges to make tabs. Wrap the strip into a cylinder, overlapping the ends ½ inch, and tape it closed. Fold the short tabs 90 degrees outward to make a narrow rim. On the mask, trim any excess toilet paper around the eye openings to open up the eye area. Insert a liner through the front of each eye, pushing it just until the rim meets the toilet paper. Do not crush the petals. On the back side, fold the tabs to meet the felt, and glue them in place. Glue sequin trim to the front rim of each eye.

5. Back mask: Trace the template onto the felt side of Stick-It Felt. Using a craft knife, cut around the perimeter and cut out the eyes. *Be sure to cut on the outer gray lines for the eyes.* Remove the release paper. Place the antennae so that the twist meets the tip of the butterfly body, and press to adhere. Stick the back mask to the felt side of the front mask.

c

6. Handle: Trim your branch to fit, and attach it to the back mask with hot glue (**c**). If you wish to add flowers, follow the instructions on pages 22-23, steps 6-7, and attach them in several locations with hot glue.

7. Headband (optional): To wear the mask hands-free, omit the branch. Cut 2 slots, about ⅛-inch wide and 1 inch apart, in the center of the back mask (forehead area). Thread it with a long length of ribbon before attaching it to the front mask. Tie the ribbon around your head with a big bow at the back.

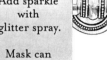

TOP TIP

Add sparkle with glitter spray.

Mask can be tinted with spray paint. Use light coats until desired shade is reached.

SKULL

1. Front mask: Copy the upper and lower skull templates. Tape the sections together on the dotted lines. Trace the template onto the felt side of Stick-It Felt. Using a craft knife, cut around the perimeter and cut out the eyes. *Be sure to cut on the inner black lines for the eyes.* Peel off the release paper.

2. Petals: Make petals from toilet paper following the instructions on pages 82 and 83, steps 1-6. Shape them as shown (a). Apply to adhesive with tweezers. Refer to the illustration above for placement guidelines. Work around the entire perimeter first, placing petals so that the tip extends slightly off the edge of the felt. Press with tweezers into the lowest folds until the petals stick. Cut 8 pieces of toilet paper into 3-inch squares. Use these to make smaller petals for 2 rows of teeth at the lower front. *Note: the adhesive is very sticky! Be careful not to lay your hand on*

a

it. Use a scrap of release paper to make a hand rest. Fill in the remaining area by overlapping and staggering the petals—and continuing to work toward the center. You may need to cut some petals shorter, or shape some wider, to fill the spaces.

3. Nose: To build the nose, shape and arrange 3 petals as shown (**b**). Glue together and set aside to dry.

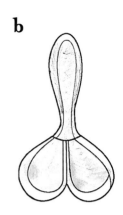

4. Eye liners: Using the template for a guide, cut 2 eye liners from medium-weight paper. Snip as marked along the lengthwise edges to make tabs. Wrap the strip into a cylinder, overlapping the ends ½ inch, and tape it closed. Fold the short tabs 90 degrees outward to make a narrow rim. On the mask, trim any excess toilet paper around the eye openings to open up the eye area. Insert a liner through the front of each eye, pushing just until the rim meets the toilet paper. Do not crush the petals. On the back side, fold the tabs to meet the felt, and glue them in place. Glue sequin trim to the front rim of each eye.

5. Back mask: Trace the template onto the felt side of Stick-It Felt. Using a craft knife, cut around the perimeter and cut out the eyes. *Be sure to cut on the outer gray lines for the eyes.* Remove the release paper, and stick the back mask to the felt side of the front mask.

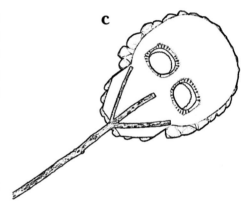

6. Glue the nose in place.

7. Handle: Trim the branch to fit, and attach it to the back mask with hot glue(**c**) .

TOP TIP

A paint stir-stick or a narrow strip of balsa wood can be used for the handle.

Copy-or-Trace
Templates

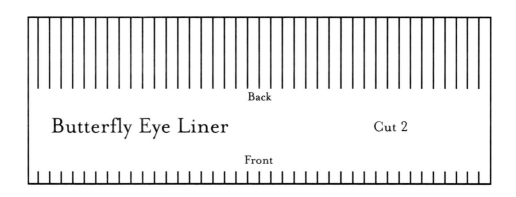

Back

Butterfly Eye Liner   Cut 2

Front

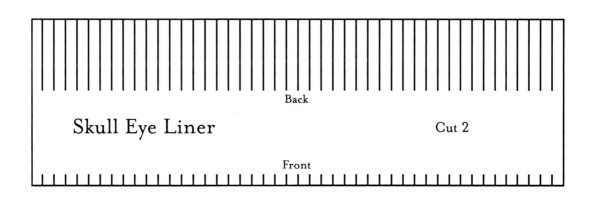

Back

Skull Eye Liner   Cut 2

Front

TOP TIP

Be sure to use
Stick-It brand
adhesive felt.
Some brands
are not stiff
enough.

Copy-or-Trace
Template

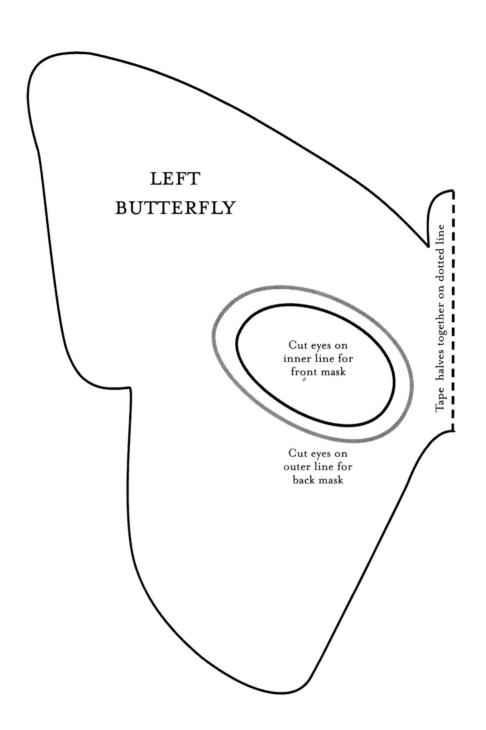

LEFT
BUTTERFLY

Cut eyes on
inner line for
front mask

Cut eyes on
outer line for
back mask

Tape halves together on dotted line

Copy-or-Trace
Template

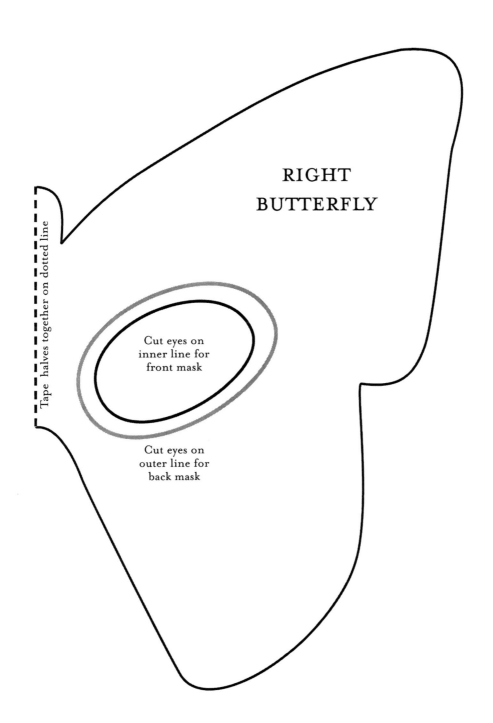

Tape halves together on dotted line

RIGHT
BUTTERFLY

Cut eyes on
inner line for
front mask

Cut eyes on
outer line for
back mask

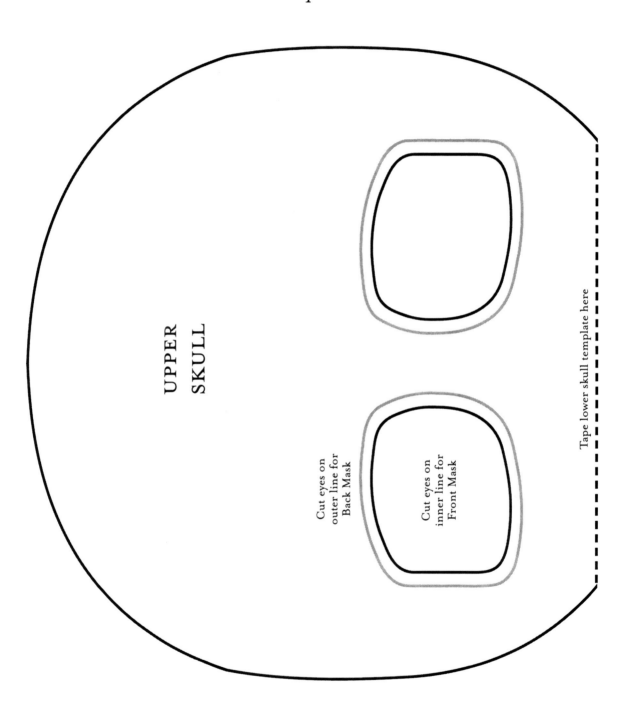

UPPER
SKULL

Cut eyes on
outer line for
Back Mask

Cut eyes on
inner line for
Front Mask

Tape lower skull template here

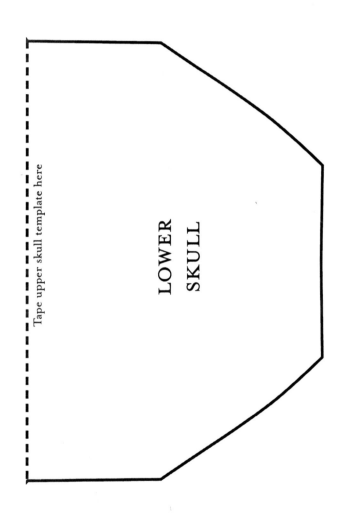

Tape upper skull template here

LOWER SKULL

PAPERWHITE WREATH

This delicate wreath is made easy with the use of a styrofoam base. For shimmer, add a light topcoat of silver glitter spray to the finished project.

Supplies: toilet paper, scissors, white floral tape, styrofoam wreath form, pencil, ballpoint pen, white glue (optional), Krylon silver glitter spray (optional)

Instructions

1. To make flowers, follow steps a-e.

a

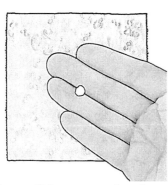

Tear off 1 square of toilet paper, and cut it into eighths. Roll one eighth into a tiny ball, and place it on a new square of toilet paper.

b

Wrap the square over the ball to encase. Compress and twist the excess toilet paper to create a stem.

c

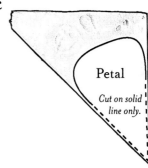

Petal

Cut on solid line only.

Tear off 1 square of toilet paper. Fold it in half diagonally 3 times until you get the shape shown above. (See page 42.) Using the petal template, cut on the solid line. Cut off the point of the petal with a very tiny snip. Unfold.

d

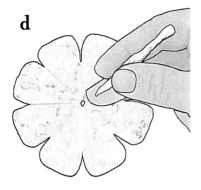

Insert the stem in the hole. It should be a tight fit. Rotate the stem—like you are screwing it into the hole. Continue until the ball meets the petal piece.

e

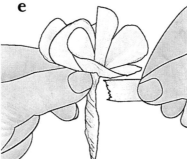

Pleat the petal piece around the stem, and secure it with floral tape. Stretch the tape as you wrap downward. Trim the stem to a length of ³⁄₄ inch.

Copy-or Trace Template

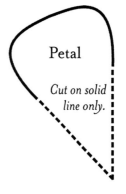

Petal

Cut on solid line only.

2. Poke a hole in the styrofoam form with a pencil, and insert the flower stem. The stem should grab onto the styrofoam and stay in place, but you can secure it further by squirting a dab of white glue in the hole before inserting the stem.

3. Continue to make and insert flowers until the wreath is full. (Spacing between pencil holes should be about 1 ¹⁄₂ to 1 ³⁄₄ inches.)

CONFETTI EGGS

Confetti eggs, or cascarones, are decorative hollow egg shells—filled with confetti, sealed with a paper cap, and used to add merriment to a festive event. The eggs are meant to be crushed in the hand above a friend's head to release a shower of confetti. Usually, the owner of the egg runs up to their friend from behind to catch them by surprise. According to Mexican folklore, having a confetti egg broken over your head is said to bring good luck. Confetti eggs lend themselves well to Easter egg hunts—even the creation of an Easter dinner centerpiece—as well as birthdays, Halloween, or weddings. In this project, brown eggs contrast nicely with the toilet paper caps.

Supplies: toilet paper, brown eggs, paring knife, skewer or toothpick, glue stick, ballpoint pen, scissors, $1/8$-inch hole punch, $3/4$-inch circular stickers, new pencil, ink pad

Instructions

1. Empty the egg: Tap on the rounded end of a raw egg with the tip of a paring knife until you make a tiny hole. Carefully grasp the blade of the paring knife (adults only) about ¼ inch from the tip **(a)**. Working your way around the hole, pinch off *very tiny* bits of shell between the knife point and your thumbnail. Continue until you have a hole the size of a dime.

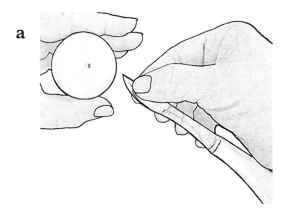

a

2. Poke into the egg with a skewer or toothpick, and stir to break up the yoke. Pour the contents into a small container, and reserve for cooking.

3. Rinse the inside of the egg with water. Zap it in a microwave oven for 20-30 seconds to dry the interior.

4. Confetti: Stack several squares of toilet paper. Cut in a crosshatch pattern at ¼-inch intervals **(b)**. Sift through the little squares with your fingers to break apart pieces that are sticking together.

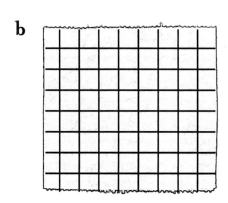

b

5. End cap: Take 1 square of toilet paper. Fold the right corner to the left side **(c)**.

c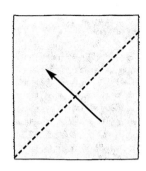

d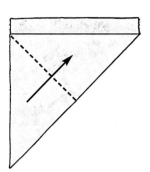

6. Fold the lower point to the right point **(d)**.

7. Fold the triangle in half **(e)**.

e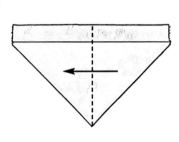

f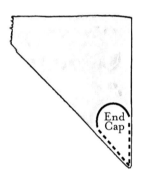

8. Align the point of the template with the lower point of the triangle **(f)**. Cut on the solid line. Unfold.

Copy-or-Trace Template

TOP TIP
Look for toilet paper in colors or prints!

9. Embellishments: The end cap may be used as is, or decorated in various ways.

g

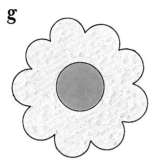

Stickers: Attach a circular sticker at the center to make a daisy.

h

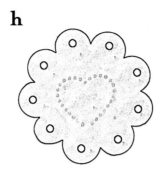

Punching: Punch a hole in the center of each scallop. For the best results, use a sharp hole punch—and hold a scrap of copy paper behind the toilet paper while punching.

i

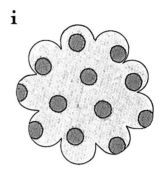

Stamping: Use the eraser of a new pencil and an ink pad to stamp dots.

10. Assembly: Fill the egg with confetti. Gently swipe a glue stick around the rim of the hole, and attach the end cap.

TOP TIP
Try white eggs for an elegant white on white effect, or color them with egg dyes before filling them with confetti.

GHASTLY GHOST

A simple wire armature—and toilet paper crumpled for texture—give this spooky fellow a puffy structure.

Supplies: toilet paper, two 18-inch pieces of 22-gauge white cloth-covered floral wire, Scotch tape, glue dots, invisible nylon thread, needle, scissors, black construction paper (or computer and printer), spooky branch

Instructions

1. Tear off three 5-square strips of toilet paper. Crumple them up—and then uncrumple them. Lay floral wire lengthwise down the center of 2 strips **(a)**. Fasten the wire in place by encasing it in Scotch tape.

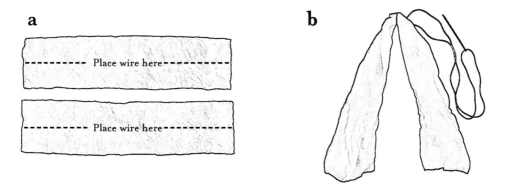

a

Place wire here

Place wire here

b

2. Cut a long piece of thread (length depending on how low you want your ghost to hang), and slip 1 end of the strand through the eye of a needle. Pull the thread through the needle until you can match up both ends. Tie and knot the doubled thread around the center of the remaining strip of toilet paper **(b)**. This will become the underskirt of your ghost.

3. Lay the wired strips—wire side down—in an X shape, matching the centers **(c)**.

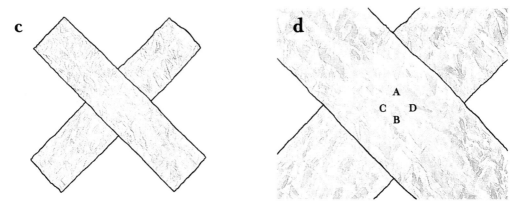

c

d

A
C   D
B

4. Secure the wires: Bring your needle up from the underside at point A. Stitch from A to B and C to D several times **(d)**. Finish stitching with the needle on the top side. Snip thread to remove the needle—leaving long thread ends.

45

5. Shape the ghost: Bend each wire downward from the center to create an inverted U shape.

6. Face: Copy and print a face template (see below) on a home printer, or trace the features onto construction paper. Cut out, and attach with glue dots.

7. Assembly: Tie a generous length of thread to a branch for hanging. Tie the ghost to the branch. Trim loose threads.

TOP TIP

Make multiple ghosts for a Ghastly Ghost mobile.

Copy-or-Trace Templates

Party Poppers
& Shakers

Make pretty party favors from toilet paper tubes. Wrap them with bath tissue and cardstock, tie with ribbon, and fill them with sweet surprises. By changing the contents to dry beans and sealing the ends, the same project becomes a fun-filled noisemaker for occasions such as New Year's Eve or July 4th.

Supplies: toilet paper, toilet paper tube, Scotch tape, glue stick, scissors, ribbon, colored cardstock, decorative hole punch, candies and small toys (poppers only), white Duck tape and dry pinto beans (shakers only)

Instructions

a

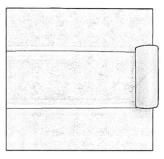

1. Tear off three 3-square strips of toilet paper. Lay them right-side down, lengthwise edges parallel—then overlap the center strip about 1 inch on top of the other 2 strips. Splice each overlap with a long strip of tape.

2. Poppers: Fill the tube with small toys, gifts, confetti, and candies. It is also fun to write greetings, holiday messages, or fortunes on small pieces of paper for inserts. Shakers: Fill the tube with dry pinto beans. Seal each end with Duck tape.

3. Align the tube with the center strip of paper (a), and roll to wrap. Tape in place. Cut 4 pieces of ribbon in contrasting colors: 2 for each end of the tube. Tie each set slowly around the toilet paper at the ends of the tube—compressing the paper as you tie. Make bows, and curl the ribbon ends. Cut fringe into the edge of the toilet paper, if desired.

4. Cut a 4-by-7-inch piece of cardstock. Punch holes equidistantly along each 7-inch edge. Align the width of the cardstock with the center of toilet paper tube, and roll to wrap. Glue in place. *To open the poppers, tug the ends simultaneously to rip the toilet paper apart.*

CUPCAKE TOPPERS & CAKE CORSAGES

Three fun projects are provided here to top a cupcake or cake. Two styles use the help of a sewing machine, while one gets a head start with a lollipop at the center. With garnishes this sweet, you'll be tempted to skip the frosting!

Supplies: 2-ply toilet paper, wooden skewers, scissors, white floral tape, sewing machine and white thread (clown or ruffle flower only), colored paper (clown only), glue stick (clown only), 1/8-inch star, circle, heart, or diamond hole punch (clown only), Scotch tape (clown only), spherical lollipops (lollipop posy only)

CLOWN

Diamond-patterned toilet paper is a perfect choice for this cheery topper.

1. Ruff: Tear off a 5-square strip of toilet paper. Fold it lengthwise, making the crease ¼ inch off-center, so that one side is slightly wider than the other **(a)**. Machine stitch ¼ inch from the foldline with a long stitch length. Pull the bobbin threads, and push the paper tightly to the center to gather.

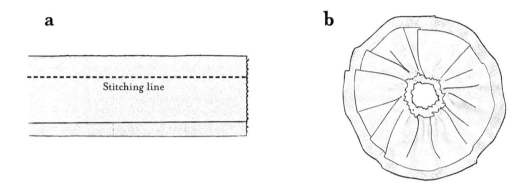

a

Stitching line

b

2. Knot all 4 threads together securely to form a circle **(b)**. Trim the thread ends to 1 inch, and conceal them under the ruffles.

3. Head: Break off a 4-inch section of skewer. Tear off a 6-square strip of toilet paper, and crumple it into a tight ball around the blunt end of the skewer **(c)**. Take a single square of toilet paper and wrap it over the ball **(d)**. Secure with floral tape **(e)**.

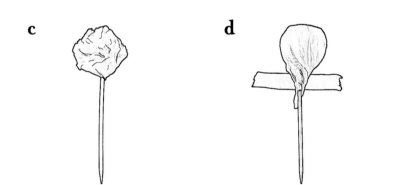

c

d

e

4. Hat: Fold 1 square of toilet paper in half, wrong sides together, so that the perforations meet (**f**).

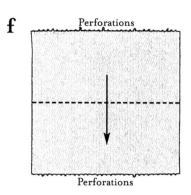

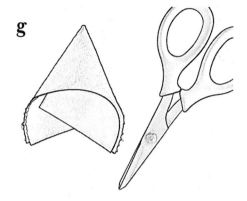

5. Roll the paper into a cone, sizing it to fit the head (**g**). Tape the cone together, and cut the bottom edge to be even.

6. Assembly: Put the hat on top of the head, and secure it at the back with tape. Punch $1/8$-inch shapes from colored paper, and glue in place for eyes. (It is helpful to grip the eyes with tweezers since they are very tiny.) Insert the skewer through the hole in the ruff. Poke it into a cupcake or cake (frosted or unfrosted)—breaking off any excess skewer as needed for a good fit. Separate both layers of paper in the ruffle, and fluff into shape.

TOP TIP
Punch clown eyes out of contact paper for instant stickers.

50

RUFFLE FLOWER

Make a fluffy flower using the same basic construction technique as the clown.

1. Ruffle: Tear off a 5-square strip of toilet paper. Fold it lengthwise, making the crease ¼ inch off-center, so that one side is slightly wider than the other. Machine stitch ¼ inch from the foldline using a long stitch length (a). Pull the bobbin threads, and push the paper tightly to the center to gather.

a

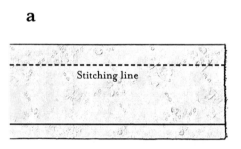

Stitching line

b

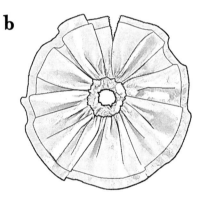

2. Knot all 4 threads together securely to form a circle (b). Trim the thread ends to 1 inch, and conceal them under the ruffles.

TOP TIP
Try this with a big lollipop for the center.

3. Center: Break off a 4-inch section of skewer. Tear off a 5-square strip of toilet paper, and crumple it into a tight ball around the blunt end of the skewer (c). Take a single square of toilet paper and wrap it over the ball (d). Secure with floral tape (e).

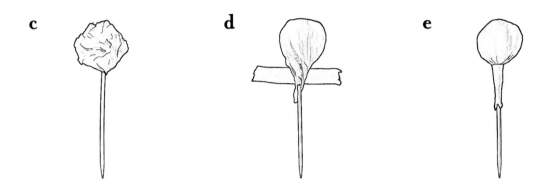

c   d   e

4. Assembly: Insert the skewer through the hole in the ruffle. Poke it into a cupcake or cake—breaking off any excess skewer as needed for a good fit. Separate all paper layers—including the plies—and fluff it into shape.

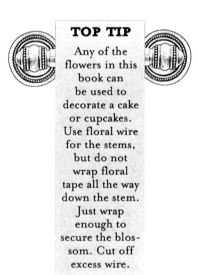

TOP TIP

Any of the flowers in this book can be used to decorate a cake or cupcakes. Use floral wire for the stems, but do not wrap floral tape all the way down the stem. Just wrap enough to secure the blossom. Cut off excess wire.

LOLLIPOP POSY

These eyecatchers feature a pop of color at the center!

1. Unwrap a lollipop. Follow the instructions for a Daisy, Cosmo, Gardenia, or Poinsettia (page 13, steps 3-6) using a lollipop for the stem and center. Wrap the base of the flower with just enough floral tape to secure the blossom. Do not wrap floral tape all the way down the lollipop stick. *Note: If your lollipop sticks are slippery, wrap the top inch with floral tape before pleating the toilet paper. This will help the paper adhere. If smaller flowers are desired, cut the petals a bit shorter than the template.*

2. Cut off any excess lollipop stick with scissors, and insert into a cupcake or cake.

FLOWER POWER

This project transforms a standard set of minilights into glowing flowers. Each bulb is surrounded with a pleated circle of toilet paper. Add electricity, and the delicate plies come to life in the light.

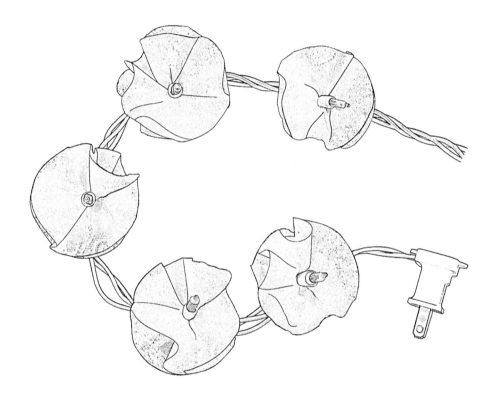

Supplies: 2-ply toilet paper, string of minilights, floral tape (same color as wire on lights), scissors, ballpoint pen

Instructions

1. Tear off 1 square of toilet paper. Fold the lower right corner to meet the left side, forming a triangle (**a**).

a

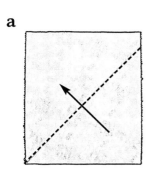

b

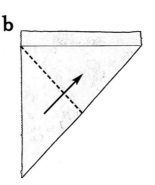

c

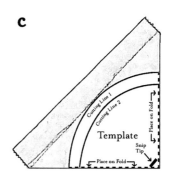

2. Fold the lower point to meet the right point (**b**).

3. Place the template as shown (**c**). Cut the raw edges of the TP into a curve following one of the cutting lines. (Choose Cutting Line 1 for a smaller flower, and Cutting Line 2 for a larger flower.) Cut off the tip with a tiny snip.

d

e

f

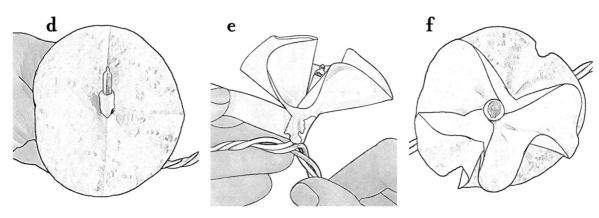

4. Insert a light bulb through the hole (**d**).

5. Pleat the paper around the base of the minilight, and secure with floral tape (**e**).

6. Separate the plies (**f**). Repeat until all lights are covered.

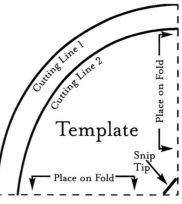

DOGWOOD BRANCH

For a dramatic element of decor, search outdoors for a branch with an interesting configuration, and embellish it with simple toilet tissue flowers. These blossoms feature a yellowish center, made by dabbing the paper with a watery mix of food coloring. Display the branch in a vase, and enjoy!

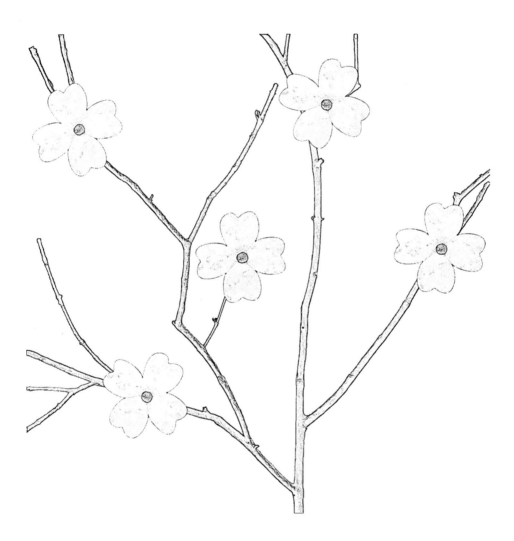

Supplies: toilet paper, tree branch, small scissors, hot glue, ballpoint pen, brown floral tape, yellow and green food coloring, Q-tips

Instructions

1. To make the flowers, follow steps a-e.

a

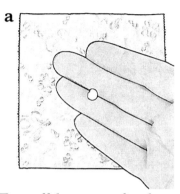

Tear off 1 square of toilet paper. Cut it into quarters. Roll 1 quarter into a ball. Place the ball on a new square of toilet paper.

b

Wrap the square over the ball to encase. Compress and twist the excess toilet paper to create a stem. Make a weak mixture of yellow or yellow-green food coloring and water. Use a Q-tip to dab it on top of the stem. Let dry.

c

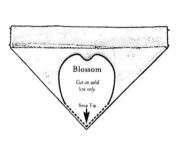

Tear off 1 square of toilet paper. Fold it in half diagonally 2 times until you get the shape shown above. (See page 55, steps 1-2.) Using the template, cut on the solid line. Cut off the point of the petal with a very tiny snip. Unfold.

d

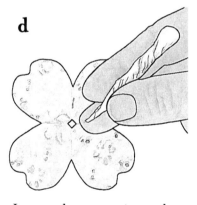

Insert the stem into the hole. It should be a snug fit. Rotate the stem as you push—like you are screwing the stem into the hole.

e

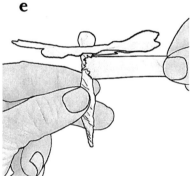

Wrap floral tape several times around the stem at the base of the flower. Stretch the tape as you wrap. Trim stem to ¼ inch.

Copy-or Trace Template

Blossom

Cut on solid line only.

Snip Tip

TOP TIP

Want bigger or smaller blossoms? Substitute the flowers from the Paperwhite Wreath or the Blossoms & Birds Mobile.

2. Attach the flower stem to the branch with hot glue. Repeat steps 1-2 to make as many blossoms as you would like.

HOLIDAY GARLANDS

The perforated-strip format of toilet paper is perfect for garlands inspired by paper dolls. Hang one on a mantel, or in a window, for a quick holiday decoration. The facial features are easily stamped with a pencil eraser and an ink pad.

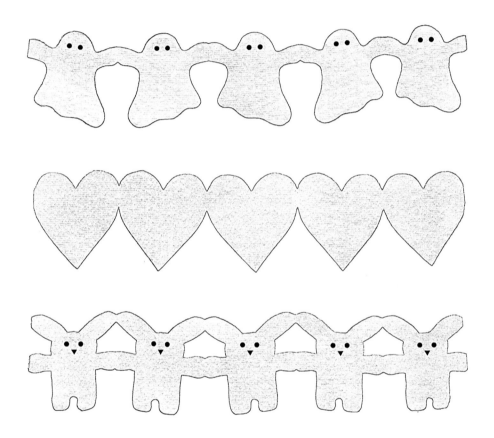

Supplies: toilet paper, ballpoint pen, scissors, Scotch tape, ink pad and new pencils (ghosts and rabbits only), knife (rabbits only), glue dots

Instructions

1. Tear off a length of toilet paper. Fan-fold it on the perforations. Trace a template on the top square with a ballpoint pen.

2. Cut along the solid lines. *Do not cut on the dotted lines.* Unfold.

3. Use a pencil eraser as a rubber stamp to print eyes on the ghost and rabbit. Use a sharp knife (adults only) to cut a pencil eraser into a triangle for the rabbit's nose.

4. For a longer garland, repeat steps 1-3, and tape the strips together. Attach to the desired surface with glue dots.

Copy-or-Trace Template

Ghost

Copy-or-Trace Template

Heart

Copy-or-Trace Template

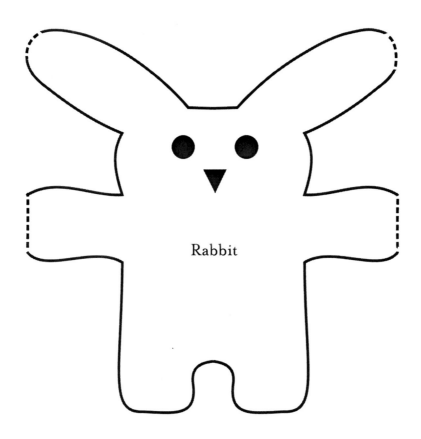

Rabbit

EMBROIDERED TOILET PAPER

Try your hand at toilet paper embroidery for a whimsical hostess, housewarming, or Paper (1st) Anniversary gift. Tuck a roll in a gift basket along with coordinating items. Stitch rolls with holiday motifs for seasonal bathroom decor. Or give one for any occasion to the person who has everything! Patterns are provided for a monogram and a lavender bouquet, but use this method for any design of your own creation.

Supplies: Charmin Basic 1-ply toilet paper, Pellon Craft Fuse, press cloth, ballpoint pen, scissors, needle, embroidery floss, crewel yarn (lavender bouquet only), glue stick, nylon netting or cellophane, Scotch tape, ribbon

Instructions

Use Charmin Basic 1-ply for its softness, strength, and stretch—along with enough translucence for an embroidery pattern to show through.

1. Tear off 1 square of toilet paper. Use it for a template to cut a piece of Pellon Craft Fuse. Place the Craft Fuse—shiny adhesive side up—on top of an embroidery template, and trace the design with a ballpoint pen. *Be careful how you orient the Craft Fuse for tracing. Refer to the illustrations on pages 62–63. When the toilet paper roll is standing on end, the embroidery motif should be positioned vertically.*

2. Take the roll of toilet paper, and unroll the first few squares. Place the Craft Fuse—shiny adhesive side down—on the wrong side of the 2nd square. Using a press cloth, a hot iron, and slight pressure, iron in place briefly until the Craft Fuse bonds.

3. Cut a piece of embroidery floss about 18-inches long. Split it into 3-strand sections. Thread a needle, and embroider your design. A hoop is not necessary. (Do not catch the first square of toilet paper in your stitches.) Iron your work with a press cloth when done.

4. Apply glue stick to the back side of the embroidery. Adhere the first square to the wrong side of the stitchery. Rewind the paper onto the toilet paper roll. Wrap with cellophane or nylon netting, pushing the bottom edges of the wrapper up into the core. Tie at the top with ribbon.

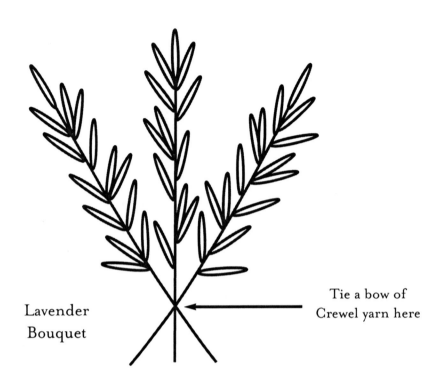

Lavender

Bouquet

Tie a bow of
Crewel yarn here

Monogram
Border

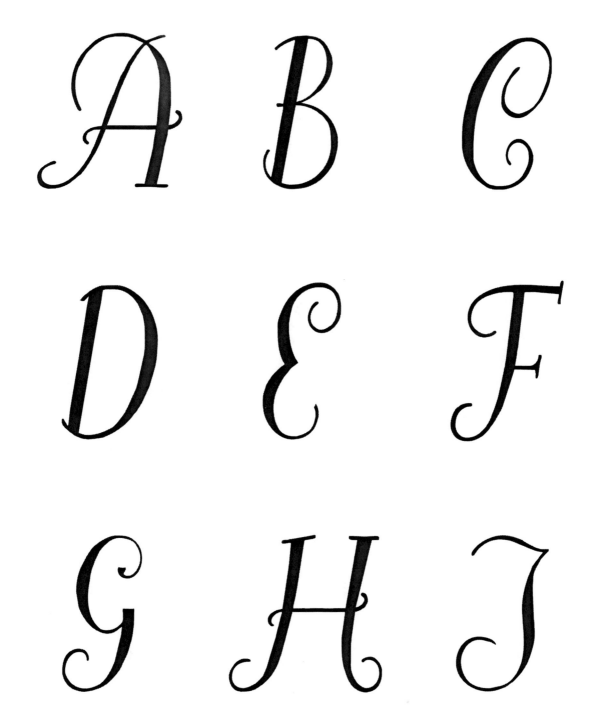

J K L

M N O

P Q R

S T U

V W X

Y Z

TOP TIP

Try toilet paper embroidery with an embroidery sewing machine. Use a thick, quality toilet paper with a stabilizer. Hoop marks can be ironed out.

TOILET PAPER CAKE

This bridal shower gift sure takes the cake! Toilet paper is as practical as it gets—but it's the presentation that makes this a hit. Pack it with extra punch by tucking small gifts, money, or gift certificates inside the toilet paper tubes. Decorate it with toilet paper flowers—or flickering LED candles—to make a great conversation piece for the day, and a fond memory long after.

Supplies: 11 regular-sized (4-inch diameter) rolls of toilet paper, 7 yards of ⅝-inch wide ribbon, wrapping paper, scissors, Scotch tape, white glue, 2 toilet paper tubes, cardboard, box cutter, skewer, pencil, string, 2 yards of 54-inch wide nylon netting, pipe cleaners (flower option), battery-operated LED flickering tealights and rubber bands (candle option),

Instructions

1. Cake Plate: Using a box cutter, cut a 14-inch diameter circle of cardboard. For a makeshift compass, cut a piece of string. Knot one end to a skewer and the other end to a pencil—setting the string length to 7 inches. Poke the skewer in the cardboard as your pivot point. Hold the skewer while pulling the pencil outward until the string is tight. Draw a circle, keeping the string tight at all times—and the pencil vertical. Cover the cardboard circle with wrapping paper. Glue a piece of ribbon around the rim. Cut three 2-inch cylinders of toilet paper tube. Wrap each with a strip of wrapping paper. Glue them equidistantly from each other on the bottom of the cardboard plate. Let the glue dry.

2. Cake: To make the bottom tier, set 1 roll of toilet paper in the center of the cake plate, and encircle it with 6 rolls. Stagger 3 rolls above the bottom tier. Place 1 roll on top. Wrap each tier with ribbon, and tie in a bow.

3. Insert small gifts, money, or gift certificates inside the toilet paper tubes, if desired.

4. Flowers: Make any of the flowers in this book to decorate the cake. Place them inside the toilet paper tubes, and tuck them around the bottom. *The sample on page 68 and on the back cover of this book was made with spray-painted roses (with pipe cleaner stems) from page 18, and leaves from page 88. The topper is a bouquet of roses—stems secured with a pipe cleaner.*

5. Candles: Another variation is to decorate your cake with battery-powered candles. Wrap rubber bands around the circumference of the candles until they are a snug fit in a toilet paper tube. Insert in the tubes until flush with the upper edge. To cover the gap between the candle and the tube, make doilies: use the Dogwood Blossom template on page 57, and follow step 1c. Push the hole in the doily down over the plastic flame. Stagger 2 or 3 doilies on each candle until you get sufficient coverage.

6. For gift-giving, wrap the cake in nylon netting, and tie it at the top with ribbon.

TOP TIP

Check your kitchen for a 14-inch pizza pan to use as a ready-made template for cutting the cake plate.

ORIGAMI ROSE PARTY FAVOR

This rose blossoms like magic from toilet paper alone. Lay one at each place setting for pretty party favors. They're amazing to make, and a joy to receive.

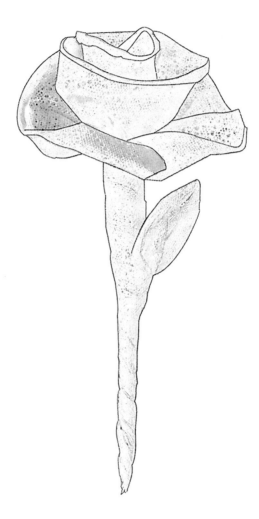

Supplies: toilet paper, hand lotion or fingertip moistener (available at office supply stores), perfume (optional)

Instructions

a

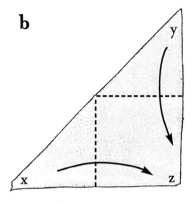

Leaf: Tear off 1 square of toilet paper. Fold point x to point y.

b

Fold points x and y to point z.

c

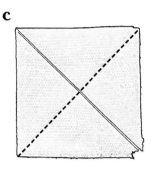

Using your fingertips, pleat your way diagonally across the square until the end points meet.

d

Twist the lower end tightly to form a stem.

e

Stem wrap: To make your stem wrap, tear off a strip of toilet paper that is 2, 3 or 4 squares long. The optimal length varies with different toilet papers, how tight you wrap, and personal prefer- ence in stem length. Try different lengths to see what you like the best.

Fold the strip in half lengthwise—then fold it in half lengthwise again.

Set it aside for later.

f

Blossom: Tear off a strip of 6 squares. Moisten your "rolling" fingertips with hand lotion or fingertip moistener. (I roll with my right thumb and index fin- ger.)

g

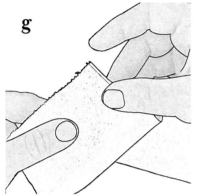

Start rolling one length-wise edge of the strip. Roll tightly, just enough to hide the raw edge.

h

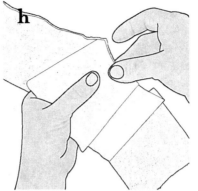

Continue rolling down the entire length of one side.

i

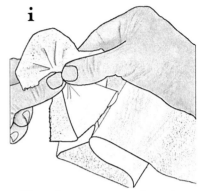

Flip the strip so that the rolled edge is facing away from you. Start shaping the rose by pleating your way down the middle of the strip, as shown.

j

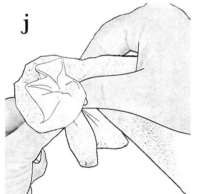

Gradually shorten the length of the strip and create fullness by pleating the paper in a push—pucker—push—pucker manner.

k

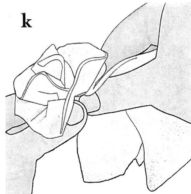

Work in a circular fashion—around and around. Shape the rose as you go.

l

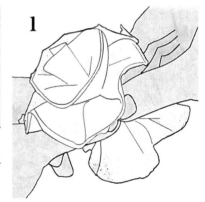

Practice makes perfect! (*It may take a few tries to get the feel of it.*)

m

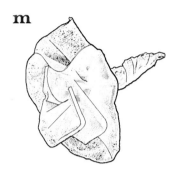

When the entire strip is pleated into a pretty flower shape, pinch and twist the bottom half to compress the paper as much as possible.

n

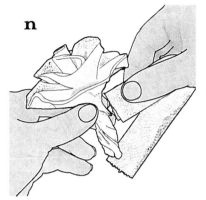

Create a stem: Place the stem wrap (from step e) at the base of the flower. Begin wrapping—tightly but gently.

o

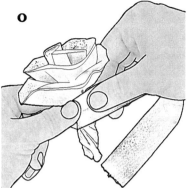

Work your way downward, spinning the flower and overlapping the wraps.

p

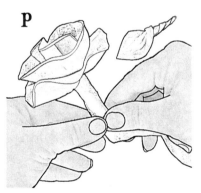

When you have wrapped 2 inches or so, the base of the flower should be covered. Now it's time to add the leaf.

q

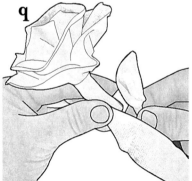

Place the leaf against the stem. Wrap over the twisted end of the leaf, then continue overlapping your wraps to create the rest of the stem.

r

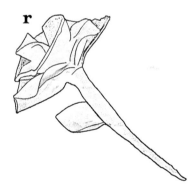

Twist the end tightly to secure it in place. For a more finished look, roll the remaining raw edges of the flower. Spray lightly with perfume, if desired.

TOILET PAPER TUBE ORNAMENTS

Use glitter and glue to transform toilet paper tubes into sparkling, elegant ornaments —fit for a tree! Make them in various jewel tones by using different colors of glitter.

Supplies: toilet paper tubes, scissors, ruler, pencil, white glue and brush or 3M Super 77 spray adhesive, hot glue, glitter, 13-by-9-inch pan, wax paper, 18-gauge wire (spiral only), table knife (filigree only), ribbon or cord (filigree only)

Instructions

SPIRAL ORNAMENT

One toilet paper tube will make 2 ornaments.

1. Toilet paper tubes have a seamline that spirals around the cylinder. Cut along the seamline, and spread the tube open. The cardboard will have the shape of a parallelogram. Cut the shape in half diagonally, and cut a curve along each side, as shown (a). Recoil each section into a spiral.

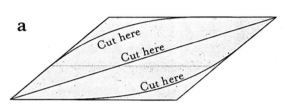

2. Hanger: Cut two 4-inch pieces of 18-gauge wire. Bend 1 end over a pencil into a hook, and stick the other end to the top of each spiral with hot glue (b).

3. Glitter: Coat the cardboard with glue by brushing it with white glue or spraying it with spray adhesive. (Avoid getting glue on hooked end of wire.) Working over a 13-by-9-inch pan lined with wax paper, sprinkle liberally with glitter. Let dry until the glue has set. Repeat the process if necessary for full glitter coverage.

FILIGREE ORNAMENT

One toilet paper tube will make 1 ornament.

1. Flatten a toilet paper tube, and crease the folds with a table knife. Cut crosswise at ³/₄-inch intervals to make 5 pieces (a).

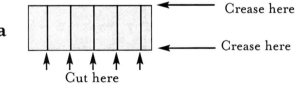

2. Open each piece into a petal shape. Place a dab of hot glue at one end of each petal, and glue all together as shown (b).

3. Apply glitter following the procedure in step 3 of Spiral.

4. Tie a piece of ribbon or cord through one of the petals for hanging.

MUMMY COSTUMES

King and Queen Mummy are quite a frightful twosome! To make these costumes, foundation garments are sprayed with adhesive and wrapped with toilet paper. Top them off with a toilet paper mask or wig. Lightly spray your work with tan spray paint for a more aged appearance.

Supplies: toilet paper, 3M Super 77 Spray Adhesive (available at craft or hardware stores), newspaper, drop cloth, foundation garments (see step 1), yardstick, clothes pins, melon or cabbage the size of your head, large oatmeal container, tan spray paint (optional)

Instructions

KING MUMMY

1. Find white clothing to use for your foundation pieces: a pair of pants, a long-sleeved shirt, and a ski mask. A sweatshirt and sweatpants would work well—or even white jeans. For an open-face version, use a hooded sweatshirt, and omit the ski mask. Shop at a thrift store, or search the web for inexpensive garment blanks. (See Resources.)

2. Prep the toilet paper: Your costume will be the most realistic with torn-edge strips. Tear off a strip of toilet paper. Lay a yardstick on top of the strip—1 inch from the edge. Press firmly on the yardstick, and use it for a guide to tear off the edge (a). Repeat on the other side. You should now have a strip that is about 2 inches wide with irregular edges. Prepare a big batch of strips in this manner. Hint: Save time by stacking strips and tearing multiple layers at a time.

a

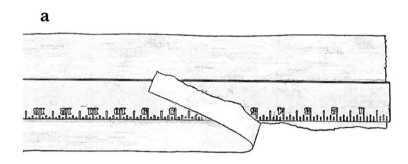

3. Fitting: Try on the shirt and pants. Mark the pants at the point where the bottom of the shirt hits them. Use colored chalk, tape, or a pin.

4. How to wrap: Work in a well-ventilated area with a drop cloth. Spray one section of garment at a time with adhesive (for example, a leg). Wrap from the bottom upward with prepped strips, and press the toilet paper into the adhesive. Overlap the strips slightly as you wrap. Allow some ends to hang loose and straggly. Place newspaper over completed areas when spraying the next area to protect finished work from overspray.

5. Shirt: Place the shirt on a hanger, and stuff it with crumpled newspaper. (Clip the hem with clothes pins, if necessary, to hold the paper in place.) Wrap as described in step 4.

6. Pants: Stuff the pants with crumpled newspaper. Hang them by the waistband from a pants hanger. Wrap as described in step 4, wrapping only the area that will be visible below the shirt.

7. Mask: Place the melon or cabbage on top of an oatmeal container for a makeshift wig form. Cover the form with a plastic grocery bag and then the ski mask. Wrap as described in step 4.

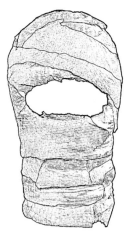

8. Accessories: Wear white gloves on your hands and large white socks over your shoes. Use black face paint around your eyes.

TOP TIP
For a different look, use a hooded sweatshirt, and omit the ski mask.

QUEEN MUMMY

Additional supplies: white Duck tape (wig only), plastic grocery bag (wig only)

1. Find white clothing to use for your foundation. Choose a form-fitting dress with simple styling. Shop at a thrift store, or search the web for inexpensive garment blanks. (See Resources.)

2. Prep the toilet paper: See step 2 for King Mummy.

3. How to wrap: See step 4 for King Mummy.

4. Dress: Place the dress on a hanger. Stuff the body and sleeves with crumpled newspaper or a piece of cardboard. Clamp the hem with clothes pins, if necessary, to contain the stuffing. Be creative when wrapping your dress, and express your individual style. Loose vertical strips at the neckline and skirt are easy and effective.

5. Wig: Place the melon (or cabbage) on top of a large oatmeal container for a makeshift wig form. Cover the melon with a plastic grocery bag, and wrap the top half with overlapping strips of white Duck tape to create a wig base. (The taped plastic will be the foundation of your wig.) Trim away the excess plastic, leaving only taped plastic in the shape of a skull cap. Prep strips of toilet paper as described in step 2 for King Mummy. Make them the length you would like for your hair. Next, tear each prepped strip in half lengthwise—so that your strips are 1 inch wide. Remove the cap from the melon, spray it with adhesive, and place it back on the melon. Start at the bottom of the cap, and attach rows of toilet paper strips all around. Adhere only the top inch of the strip to the adhesive. Continue filling the cap with strips until it is covered. Trim as desired to make bangs or layers.

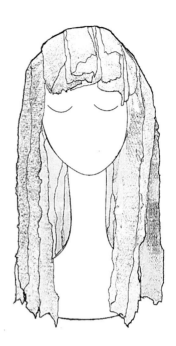

6. Optional accessories: Cover a purchased half-mask with horizontal strips of prepped toilet paper. Wrap long ragged strips of toilet paper around your upper arms, tape in place, and let them dangle. In place of a wig, wrap strips of toilet paper around your forehead.

TOP TIP
Spray costumes lightly with tan spray paint for an aged appearance.

GIFT GARNISHES

Great gift wrapping is the perfect occasion to express your creativity. By trimming packages with a unique ornament, even simple gifts can be personalized with flair. Pretty packages also make lovely mantle or tabletop decor.

Supplies: toilet paper, scissors, Krylon silver glitter spray (optional), additional supplies as listed for individual projects

Instructions

Measurements are provided for each garnish to help you find the best fit for your gift.

GIANT MUM

10 inch diameter

Crisp 2-ply toilet paper is a must for success.
Choose one made from 100% recycled paper.

Additional supply: curling ribbon

1. Tear off six 3-square strips of toilet paper. Stack them on top of each other, and fan-fold lengthwise into 4 equal sectons **(a)**.

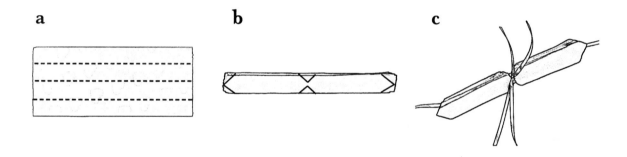

a   b   c

2. Fold the strip in half widthwise to locate the center, and unfold. Cut notches at the center. Cut both ends into points **(b)**.

3. Cut 3 pieces of curling ribbon. Lay 1 piece lengthwise under the toilet paper strip. (This will be used to tie the flower onto a package.) Tie the remaining 2 pieces securely around the center **(c)**. Trim the ends, and curl them tightly.

4. Gently separate the layers of toilet paper—and their plies. (Work close to the center to avoid breaking through the perforations.) Apply glitter spray, if desired.

 TOP TIP

All of the flowers on pages 8-18 are similar in size to a standard bow and can be used to garnish a gift.

KANZASHI FLOWER

4 inch diameter

To shape this elegant gift topper, individual squares of toilet paper are folded into petals, strung together, and tied into a circle. A center piece is glued on top for the finishing touch.

Additional supplies: needle, thread, cardboard, hot glue, straight pins

1. Petals: Tear off 1 square of toilet paper. Lay it right side down. Fold the lower right corner to left side **(a)**. (These petals are very forgiving. It doesn't matter that toilet paper squares aren't perfectly square.)

a

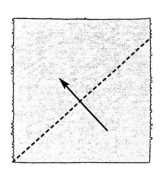

b

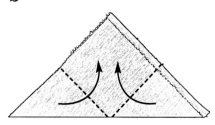

2. Fold the left and right points to the top point **(b)**.

c

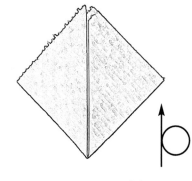

d

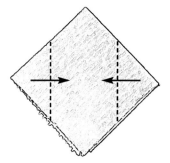

3. Flip the piece vertically **(c)**.
4. Fold the left and right points to the center **(d)**.

5. Fold the piece in half lengthwise (e).

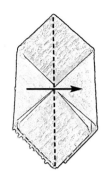

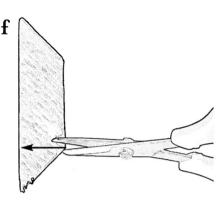

6. Trim to straighten the raw edges, starting flush with the bottom of the shortest folds (f).

7. Pinch the cut end, push down on the tip, and run a finger around the inner rim to make a rounded petal (g). Refer to the illustration on page 82 or the photo on the back cover of this book for the shape. (Illustrations g and h show the right side of the petal.)

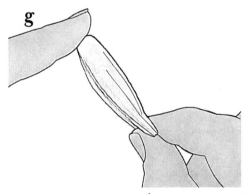

8. Insert a straight pin (or use a clothes pin) at the base of the petal to hold the folds in place until final assembly (h).

TOP TIP

Get creative and add color with different center pieces such as buttons, stickers, circles of wrapping paper, confetti dots, or faux gemstones.

9. Repeat steps 1-8 to make 7 more petals (or as many as you need to make a full flower with your particular toilet paper). Thread a needle with double thread. Take a petal, remove the pin, and insert the threaded needle about ¼ inch from the raw edges and centered across the width, as shown **(i)**. One by one, string all petals onto the thread in this manner—right side facing up **(j)**.

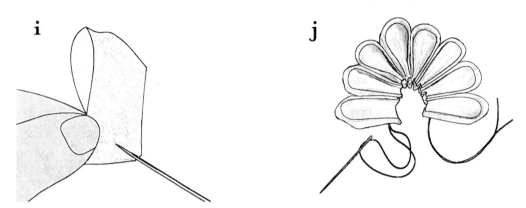

10. Cut the thread near the needle—and remove the needle. Tie all threads together in a double knot. Don't tie too tightly: the circle of petals should have a small hole at the center **(k)**. Pull the thread ends to the back of the flower, and trim.

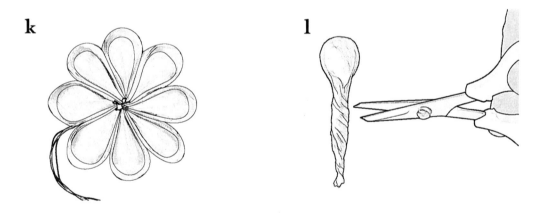

11. Center piece: Tear off 3 squares of toilet paper. Crumple 2 into a ball and wrap them with the 3rd. Pinch and twist the raw edges into a stem. Trim the stem length to ½ inch **(l)**.

12. Cut a circle of cardboard about 2 inches in diameter. (A spice jar makes a good template.) Fasten the circle to the center back of the flower with hot glue. This will give the flower stability. Fill the hole in the center front with hot glue. Insert the stem of the center piece. Apply glitter spray, if desired. Attach to a gift box or bag with double-stick tape or glue dots.

MONEY ROLL

This toilet paper roll cleverly conceals a bundle of cash! It's an unforgettable way to present money to children, graduates, or anyone—for any occasion. Intersperse handwritten notes with the bills to add sentiment appropriate to the occasion. Everyone will enjoy watching the recipient unwind an entire roll to cash in on their gift. Giving money doesn't get any more fun than this!

Additional supplies: cash, wrapping paper or cellophane, copy paper (optional)

Unwind a roll of toilet paper until you are near the core. It is easiest to do this by placing the roll on a table and letting the toilet paper flow onto the floor. Rewind the roll and insert cash at intervals. Wind evenly so that the roll looks new. Cut pieces of paper the same size as money, write notes that are appropriate for the occasion, and insert them randomly, if desired. Leave the front end of the toilet paper roll empty for a few winds so that the recipient doesn't start reaching money right away. Wrap the stuffed roll in wrapping paper or cellophane, tucking the edges of the wrapper into the cardboard core.

TOP TIP
Return money roll to original toilet paper packaging for a gift in disguise.

HERE'S MY HEART

2 inch diameter

*Simple and chic, this topper is
the perfect way to say "I love you".*

Additional supply: Scotch tape

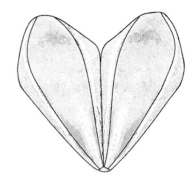

1. Petals: Tear off 1 square of toilet paper, and lay it right side down. Fold the lower right corner to the left side **(a)**. (These petals are very forgiving. It doesn't matter that toilet paper squares aren't perfectly square.)

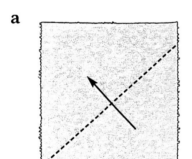

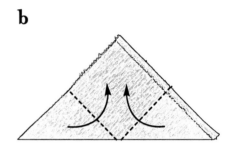

2. Fold the left and right points to the top point **(b)**.

3. Flip the piece vertically **(c)**.

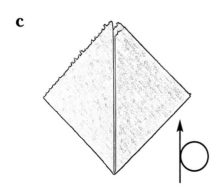

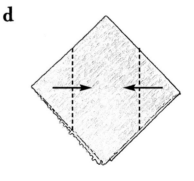

4. Fold the left and right points to the center **(d)**.

5. Fold your work in half lengthwise (e).

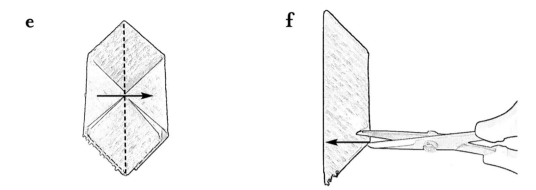

6. Trim to straighten the raw edges, starting flush with the bottom of the shortest folds (f). Repeat steps 1-6 to make another petal.

7. Position the petals as shown, pinch them together at the raw edges, and attach them with Scotch tape (g). This is the right side of the heart. Flip the piece over.

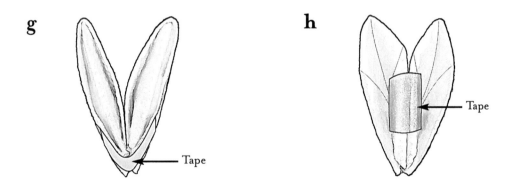

8. Tape the petals together along the center folds (h). Turn back to the right side, push down on the tips of petals, and run a finger around the inner rims to create a heart shape. Apply glitter spray, if desired. Attach to a package with hot glue, double-stick tape, or a 3M foam mounting square.

ROLLED ROSE

2 ½ inches by 3 ½ inches

Additional supply: glue dots

So easy, yet so pretty, this decoration is delightful for a small gift.

1. Blossom: Tear off a 2-square strip of toilet paper. Fold ½ inch under on each end. Fold the strip in half lengthwise **(a)**.

2. Roll the paper widthwise (folded edge up), rolling the first inch tightly, then continue by wrapping loosely, and pleating the paper as you go **(b)**.

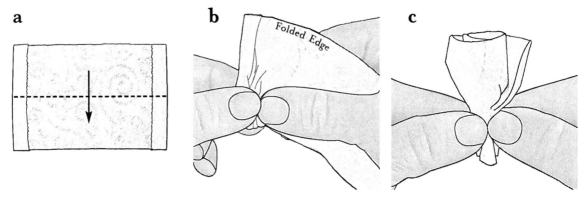

a

b

Folded Edge

c

3. Pinch and twist the bottom of the flower to create a stem **(c)**. Secure with Scotch tape. Trim the stem end at an angle, just as you would trim a fresh rose for a vase.

4. Leaf: Tear off 1 square of toilet paper, and narrowly trim the perforations off of the edges. Fold the square in half diagonally **(d)**.

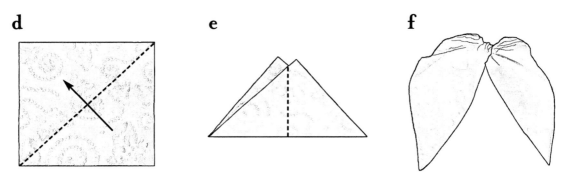

d

e

f

5. Pinch the paper to compress the center of the triangle, and give it a twist **(e)**. Using a glue dot, attach leaves to the top of the flower where the blossom meets the stem. To create a cluster, make 2 more roses to attach on top.

ORIGAMI BUTTERFLY

3 inches by 8 inches

Try this fluttery finish for a cheerful way to embellish a box.

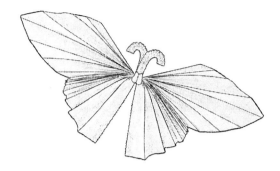

Additional supply: pipe cleaner

1. Upper wings: Tear off a 2-square strip of toilet paper. Fold and unfold lengthwise to make a crease. Fold all 4 corners to meet the crease **(a)**.

a

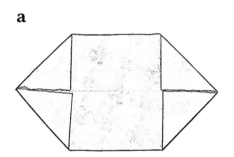

b

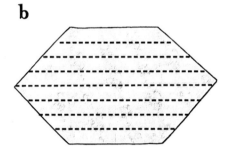

2. Flip your work over. Fan-fold your way lengthwise across the entire piece, making the folds about ½ inch wide **(b)**.

3. Lower wings: Tear off a 2-square strip of toilet paper. Fan-fold it widthwise in ½-inch folds.

4. Assembly: Stack the upper wings on top of the lower wings. Wrap a pipe cleaner around the center of the wing stacks, and twist it at the top. Cut the pipe cleaner tips to a length you like for the antennae, and bend the ends into curls. Fan out the lower wings. Apply glitter spray, if desired.

CLASSIC BOW

7 ½ inch diameter

Additional supplies: ribbon, clothes pins

1. Tear off three 5-square strips of toilet paper.

2. Lay 1 strip right side down. Fold the right and left squares inward, stacking them directly on top of the middle square to make a loop **(a)**.

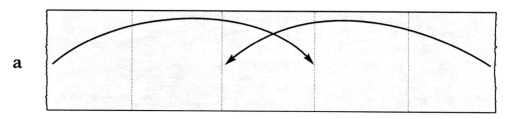

3. Pinch the paper together at the center of the loop **(b)**. Insert your fingers in each side of the loop, and gently puff up the paper.

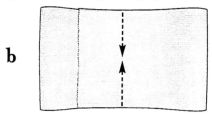

4. Hold the pleats in place with a clothes pin **(c)**. Repeat steps 2-4 with the remaining strips.

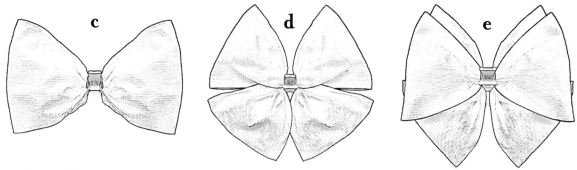

5. Place 2 loops side-by-side, and clamp them together at the center with a clothes pin **(d)**. Place the 3rd loop on top, and hold it in place with a clothes pin **(e)**. Cut a piece of ribbon. Remove clothes pin, and tie all loops together with ribbon.

PINWHEEL BOW

7 1/2 inch diameter

Additional supply: ribbon

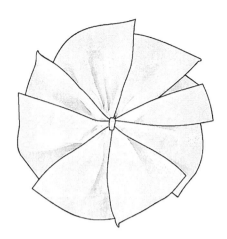

1. Cut an 18-inch piece of ribbon, and set it aside.

2. Tear off four 2-square strips of toilet paper, and stack them up. Cut the ends at a slight angle, sloping from the corner to 1/2 inch into the opposite side **(a)**.

a

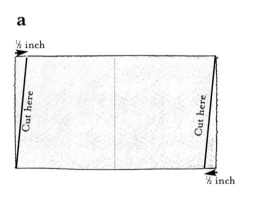

½ inch

Cut here

Cut here

½ inch

TOP TIP

Need an extra hand? Use a clothes pin to hold your work.

~

Add more toilet paper strips for increased fullness.

3. Take the strips 1 at a time, and pinch the paper along the perforation line **(b)**. Align the strips side-by-side, and tie them together at the center with ribbon **(c-d)**.

b   **c**   **d**

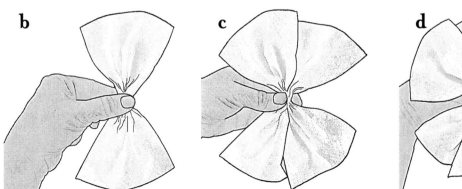
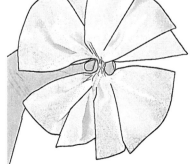

4. Arrange the petals into a pretty pinwheel shape.

STARBURST BOW

11 inch diameter

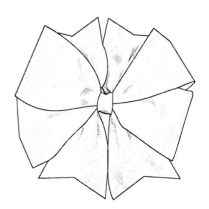

Additional supply: Scotch tape, ribbon

1. Cut two 18-inch pieces of ribbon, and tear off 1 square of toilet paper. Set the items aside.

2. Tear off two 3-square strips of toilet paper. Fold them loosely in half lengthwise—do not crease—and cut the ends at an angle **(a)**. Set aside.

a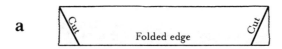

3. Tear off a 14-square strip of toilet paper. Pinch the paper together at the 1st and 4th perforations, and bring the perforations together to make a 6-inch loop **(b)**. (The pinched area will be the center of the bow.) On the long trailing end, pinch the 3rd perforation from the center, and bring it up to the center to make the lower loop **(c)**. Repeat to make 2 more loops. Tie tightly at the center with ribbon.

b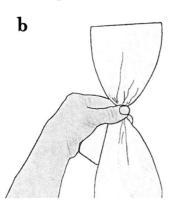

c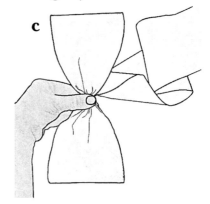

4. Pinch the reserved strips at the middle, and arrange 1 at each side of the bow. Tie them in place with ribbon.

5. Take the single square. Fold it in half, and fold it in half again (parallel to the first fold), to make a 1-by-4-inch rectangle. Wrap the rectangle around the center of the bow, and tape it in place.

92

FLORIST BOW

11 by 16 inches

Additional supply: ribbon

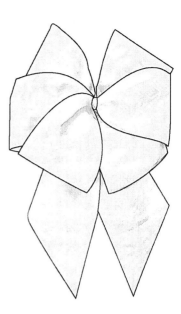

1. Cut an 18-inch piece of ribbon, and set it aside.

2. Tear off a 20-square strip of toilet paper. Pinch the paper together at the 1st and 4th perforations, and bring the pinches together to make a 6-inch loop **(a)**. (The pinched area will be the center of the bow.)

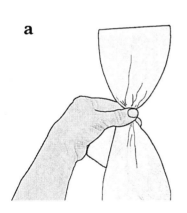

a

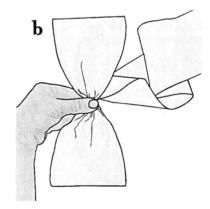

b

3. On the long trailing end, pinch the 3rd perforation from the center, and bring the pinch up to the center to make the lower loop **(b)**. Repeat the process to make 3 loops on each side, alternating sides after each loop. Tie tightly at the center with ribbon.

4. Tear off a 6-square strip of toilet paper, and pinch it at the center. Tie it to the back of the bow to make tails. Trim the tails with diagonal cuts.

CYLINDER GIFT BOX

Recycled toilet paper tubes make festive boxes for small gift items such as jewelry, lipstick, cash, or checks.

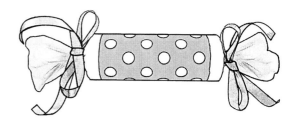

Additional supplies: toilet paper tube, ribbon, wrapping paper

1. Tear off three 3-square strips of toilet paper. Lay them right side down, lengthwise edges parallel. Overlap the center strip about 1 inch on top of the other 2 strips. Splice each overlap with a long strip of tape (a).

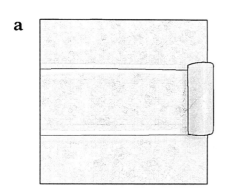

a

2. Insert your gift in the toilet paper tube. Align the tube with the center strip of toilet paper, and roll to wrap. Tape in place.

3. Cut 2 pieces of curling ribbon. Tie a piece slowly around the toilet paper at each end of tube, compressing the paper as you tie. Make a bow, and curl the ribbon ends loosely.

4. Cut a 5-by-7-inch piece of wrapping paper. Fold each lengthwise edge under—about ½ to ¾ inch. This is to give the edge a nice finish. Be sure the strip will still be wide enough to cover the splices on the toilet paper. Align the width of the wrapping paper with the center of the toilet paper tube, and roll to wrap. Tape in place.

GIFT TAGS

Flattened toilet paper tubes make terrific cardstock for tags. For a fancy finish, dress them up with decorative hole punches, faux gemstones, sequins, glitter, rubber stamps, or paper cut-outs.

Additional supplies: toilet paper tube, iron, hole punch, ribbon or twine

1. Cut lengthwise through an empty toilet paper tube. Iron it flat with a hot steam iron (cotton setting) to reveal a rectangle.

2. Cover the cardboard with colored paper (using a glue stick), if desired, or leave it as-is for a rustic look. Folded tags: fold the rectangle in half widthwise for a book-style tag. Use a table knife to crease the fold. Flat tags: cut the cardboard into a decorative shape. Trace a cookie cutter, or use a template from page 107.

3. Punch a hole at the top, and thread it with ribbon or twine. Embellish as desired.

Snowflakes

Easy and enchanting, paper snowflakes make any room look magical. The semi-translucence and ornamental embossing of toilet paper make these extra special. Attach them randomly to windows with petroleum jelly, or glue them to a card or package, and watch the magic unfold!

Supplies: toilet paper, small scissors

Instructions

1. Tear off 1 square of toilet paper. Fold the lower right corner to the left side (a).

a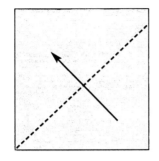

b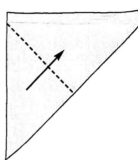

2. Fold the lower point of the triangle to the right point (b).
3. Fold the triangle in thirds, folding 1 side to the front, and 1 to the back (c).

c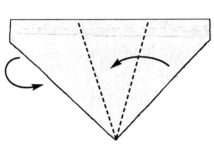

d

4. Trim across the upper edge so that all layers are even (d).
5. Cut notches or curved shapes into all edges of the triangle. Snip off the tip if you wish. See some examples below.

e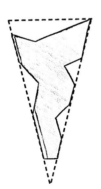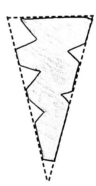

6. Unfold. Apply dots of petroleum jelly to the wrong side of the snowflake with a Q-tip, and press against a window. Snowflakes can also be attached to a card or package with a glue stick.

TOILETREE

Stitch strips of toilet paper with your sewing machine, gather them into ruffles, and pin them to a styrofoam cone. Top it off with silver glitter spray for a stunning holiday centerpiece.

Supplies: toilet paper, sewing machine, white thread, scissors, ballpoint pen, 15-inch styrofoam cone, corsage pins, white cloth-wrapped floral wire, Krylon silver glitter spray (optional)

Instructions

1. Tear off strips of toilet paper in the following lengths: 11 squares, 10 squares, 8 squares, 7 squares, 6 squares, 5 squares, and 4 squares.

2. Set aside the 4-square strip, and gather the others as follows: Machine stitch with a long stitch length, ¼ inch from one lengthwise edge. Stitch again, ¼ inch from the first stitching line. Pull the bobbin threads while pushing the toilet paper toward the middle of the strip to make ruffles. Tie the threads at one end of the strip in a double knot and trim the thread ends. Leave the threads loose at the other end for fitting on the tree.

3. The ruffles will be attached to the cone from the bottom working upward. Place the 11-square strip 3 ½ inches from the bottom of the styrofoam cone. Adjust the gathers to fit, and attach with pins. Knot and trim the threads. Place the 10-square strip of ruffles 2 inches above the previous row, adjust the gathers to fit, and attach it with pins. Knot and trim the threads. Continue in this manner, attaching the next 4 consecutively smaller strips of ruffles 2 inches above the prior row.

4. The final strip of ruffles must be tailored to fit the remaining styrofoam. Take the 4-square strip that was set aside in step 2, and fold under approximately ½ inch along one lengthwise edge. *Note: this measurement was taken using toilet paper that is 4 ¼ inches wide. You may need to adjust the fold if your toilet paper is narrower or wider than this. The goal is to have the lower edge of the top strip 2 inches above the lower edge of the previous strip.* Sew along the folded edge to gather and prepare the strip as described in step 2. Pin in place to cover the remaining styrofoam.

5. To make the topper, tear off 4 separate squares of toilet paper, and stack them up. Fan-fold the stack from one perforated edge to the other in 4 equal folds. Cutting on the solid lines only, use the template (below) to cut the ends and notches. Wrap wire around the center, and twist the ends to secure. Unfold the fan. Gently separate the layers (but not the plies), and fluff into shape. Trim the wire ends to 2 inches, and insert in tree top.

6. Coat the entire tree lightly with glitter spray, if desired.

TOP TIP

Make any size ToileTree with this formula: Use 1 square of toilet paper per inch of circumference. For example, to make ruffles for a section of cone that is 17 inches around, use 17 squares of toilet paper.

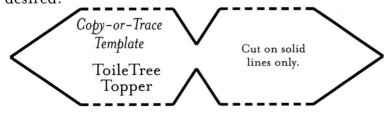

Copy-or-Trace Template

ToileTree Topper

Cut on solid lines only.

BUTTERFLY NAPKIN RING

Four squares of toilet paper, a slice of toilet paper tube, and a few more simple supplies make this charming napkin ring—and a project that is packed with mix-and-match opportunities. Stand a napkin ring on end to make an adorable Easter egg holder. Browse the flowers in this book for alternate napkin ring embellishments. Or enjoy using this butterfly in other ways, for instance, to garnish a gift or make a mobile.

Supplies: toilet paper, toilet paper tube, scissors, craft knife, pipe cleaner, hot glue, wrapping paper, Scotch tape, Krylon silver glitter spray (optional)

Instructions

1. Tear off 1 square of toilet paper and lay it right side down. Fold the lower right corner to the left side (**a**). It doesn't matter that TP squares aren't perfectly square.

a

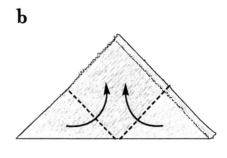

b

2. Fold the left and right points to the top point (**b**).
3. Flip the piece vertically (**c**).

c

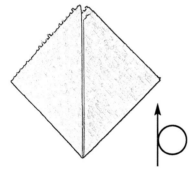

d

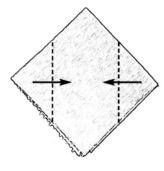

4. Fold the left and right points to the center (**d**).
5. Fold the piece in half lengthwise (**e**).

e

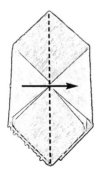

f

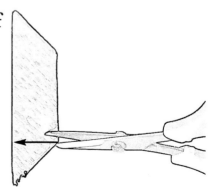

6. Trim to straighten the raw edges, starting flush with the bottom of the shortest folds (**f**). Repeat steps 1-6 to make another petal.

7. Position the petals as shown, pinch together at the raw edges, and attach with Scotch tape (**g**). This is the right side of the wings. Flip the piece over.

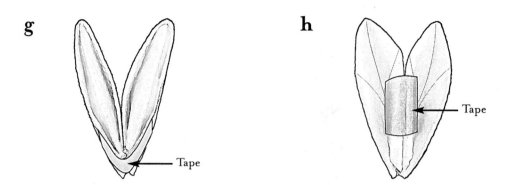

8. Tape the petals together along the center folds (**h**). Turn back to the right side. This is 1 set of wings. Repeat steps 1-8 to make a 2nd set.

9. Attach the sets of wings together at the center with hot glue (**i**). Let the glue set. Shape the wings by pushing on the tips of the petals and running your finger inside the rim. Refer to the illustration on page 100 or the photograph on the back cover of this book for the shape.

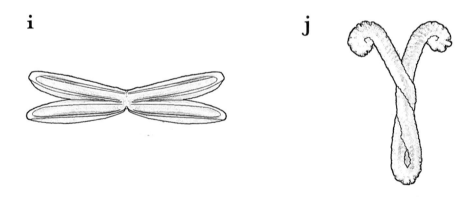

10. Butterfly body: Cut a 6-inch piece of pipe cleaner. Fold it in half, twist it together at the center, and curl the ends (**j**). Attach it over the seam of the wing sections with hot glue. Lightly coat the butterfly with glitter spray, if desired.

11. Using a craft knife, cut a 1-inch slice of toilet paper tube. Cut a 1-by-6½-inch piece of wrapping paper. Tape the wrapping paper around the slice of cardboard tube. Attach the butterfly over the taped area with hot glue. Repeat to make as many napkin holders as needed.

Paper Truffles

*For a dramatic dinner presentation, make slip-on crowns
to garnish bone tips on poultry legs, chops, or ribs.
Add them to your dish just before serving.*

Supplies: toilet paper, Scotch tape, scissors

Instructions

1. Take a 2-square strip of TP, and fold it in half along the perforations **(a)**.

a 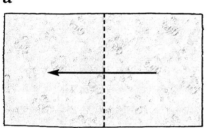   **b**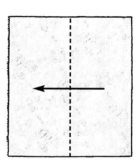

2. Fold it in half again, parallel to the first fold, but do not crease **(b)**.

3. Cut slits halfway into the softly folded edge at ½-inch intervals **(c)**.

c 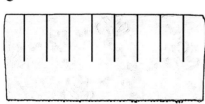   **d**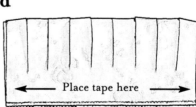

Place tape here

4. Stick a piece of Scotch tape along the uncut edge of one side **(d)**. This will act as a moisture barrier.

5. With the taped side facing inward, roll the strip into a cylinder large enough to accommodate the bones you will be embellishing. Tape the loose end closed. Insert your little finger or a teaspoon handle into the loops to puff them up.

ROSETTE BROOCH

Use your sewing machine and soft toilet paper to craft a quick and quirky corsage. Choose a premium bath tissue, and it will look like fine fabric!

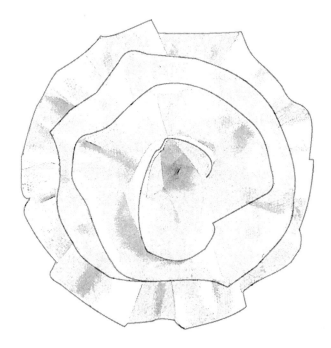

Supplies: toilet paper, sewing machine, needle, thread, scissors, felt, pin back, hot glue

Instructions

1. Blossom: Tear off a 6-square strip of toilet paper and lay it right side down. Fold ½ inch inward along the right and left ends to hide the perforations (a).

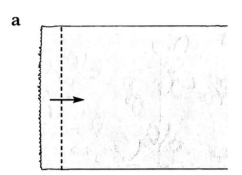

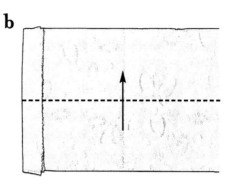

2. Fold the strip in half lengthwise, wrong sides together (b).

3. Machine stitch ¼ inch from the raw edges with a long stitch length (c). Pull the bobbin threads, and push the paper to the center to form tight gathers (d).

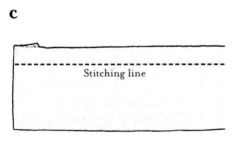

Stitching line

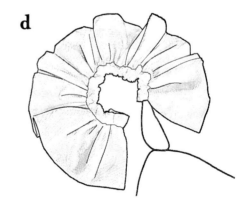

4. At each end, knot the pair of threads securely to keep the gathers taut and form a ruffled strip.

TOP TIP

Pin a brooch to the front of a card for a gift.

5. Roll the strip widthwise to form a blossom (**e**).

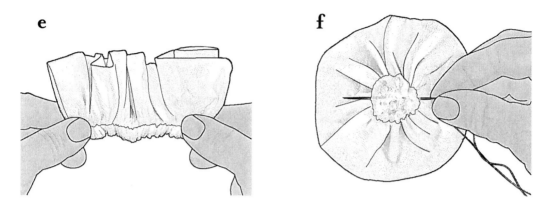

e   f

6. Hand stitch the bottom of the blossom together by driving a needle through the entire diameter at several points (**f**).

7. Base: Repeat steps 1 -3 to make a second ruffled strip. *Variation: for a more compact brooch, cut ½ inch off of the lengthwise raw edges (at step 2) before stitching.*

8. Tie all 4 threads together securely to form a circle of ruffles (**g**).

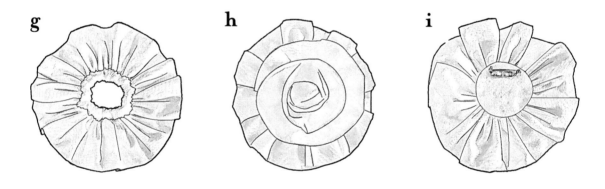

g   h   i

9. Assembly: Hot glue the bottom of the blossom into the hole in the base (**h**). Tack the loose end of the blossom to the flower with a dot of glue.

10. Using a small jar (such as a spice jar) for a pattern, cut a circle of felt. Hot glue it to the center back (**i**). Hot glue a pin back to the felt, placing it in the upper half of the circle.

106

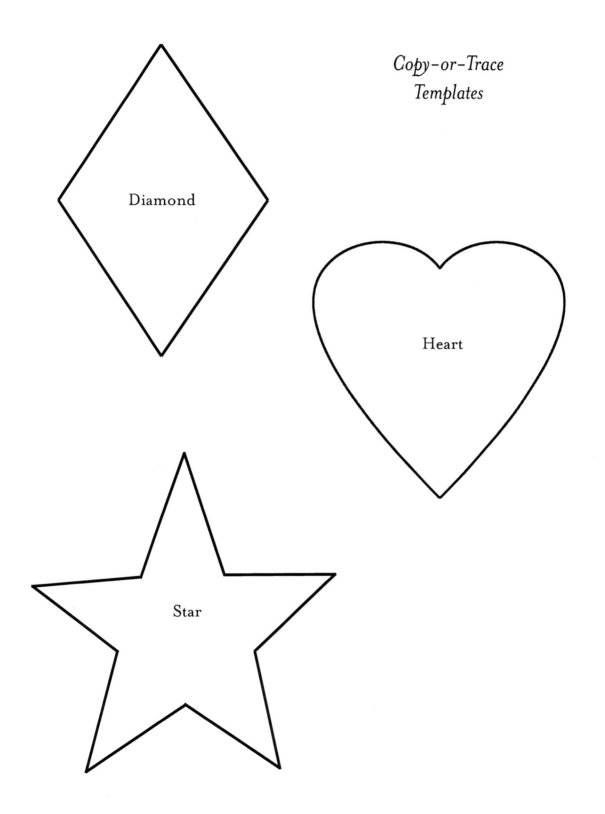

Copy-or-Trace
Templates

Diamond

Heart

Star

HOMEMADE PAPER
ORNAMENTS, SACHETS & GIFT TAGS

For a fun project to do with children, shake up a strip of toilet paper in a jar of water, turn it into pulp, and create a surprisingly sturdy new material. The rustic texture of handmade paper is charming on its own, or glitter can be added for sparkle. Sprinkle the shapes with essential oil or perfume to make sachets. Write on them to make personalized ornaments and gift tags—or hang them as is.

Supplies: toilet paper, jar with lid, sieve, paper plate, wax paper, scissors, ballpoint pen, hole punch, ribbon, glitter or food coloring (optional), cookie cutters (optional), perfume or essential oil (sachet only)

Instructions

1. Tear off 10 squares of toilet paper. Put them in the jar, and cover them with water. Add glitter or food coloring, if desired. Put the lid on tightly, and shake until the paper has turned into a slushy pulp: 100 shakes will do it.

2. Pour the mixture into a sieve over a sink. Make a thin, flat layer, and press down to remove as much water as possible. If your fingers stick to the pulp, cover it with wax paper while pressing.

3. Turn the disk of pulp out onto a paper plate, and allow it to dry overnight. If you have not added metallic glitter, you can speed the drying process in a microwave oven: heat on medium-low for 1 minute and check. Continue to heat at 1- or 2-minute intervals until dry.

4. Press a cookie cutter into the paper firmly enough to make an impression, or draw an outline using a template from page 107. Cut out the shape with scissors. Punch a hole for hanging, and tie a ribbon through the hole.

5. Sachet: place 1 or 2 drops of perfume or essential oil on the back side.

6. Gift Tag: Write a name on the paper with a pen or marker.

TOP TIP
For a freeform circular ornament, shape the wet pulp into a circle and omit step 4.

LOVELY LEI

Create a lush lei by snipping and rolling long lengths of toilet paper, then stringing them onto a central thread. For a beautiful effect, touches of color can be added to the tips. Plan on a 40-inch length for a neck lei, and 21 ½ inches for an average adult head lei.

Supplies: toilet paper, large sewing needle, heavy duty thread, scissors, hand lotion or fingertip moistener (available at office supply stores), watercolor paint or food coloring and Q-tips (optional)

Instructions

1. Thread a needle—making sure your thread is a good bit longer than the desired length of your lei. Roll up a square of toilet paper and tie it to one end **(a)**. This makes a stopper to keep your paper in place while you work.

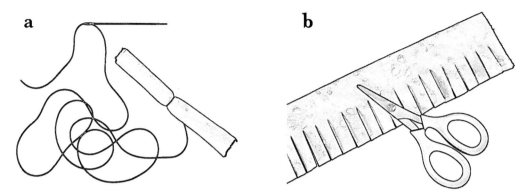

2. Tear off a generous length of toilet paper. Fold it in half lengthwise. Snip halfway across the width at ³/₈-inch intervals along the entire strip **(b)**. Unfold.

3. Moisten your fingertips with hand lotion or fingertip moistener. Twist the snips along one side into tight rolls **(c)**.

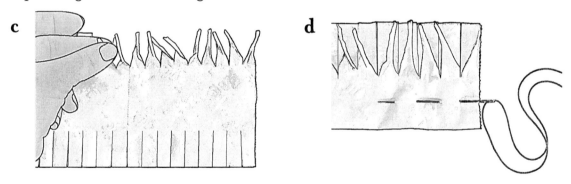

4. Refold the strip along the crease line. Sew by hand with a running stitch ½ inch from the folded edge **(d)**. Avoid passing the needle through the perforations.

5. When the entire strip is on the thread, push the paper gently toward the knotted end, twisting as you push to create a full, rounded shape. Repeat steps 2-5 until you have enough length. Cut the stopper off, and knot the threads from each end together.

8. Color (optional): Add touches of color with a watery mix of food coloring or watercolor paint. Dab lightly with a Q-tip onto the ends of the fringes, and let the water absorb to spread the color.

ROSEBUD PLACE CARDS

Make place cards your guests will never forget—and get the conversation rolling—with tiny origami rosebuds made from a single square of toilet paper!

Supplies: toilet paper, cardstock, copy paper, double-stick tape, craft knife, tweezers, pen

Instructions

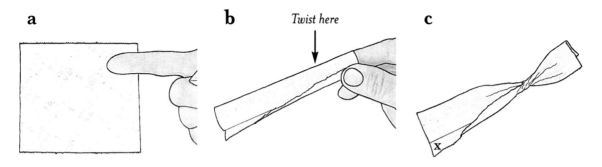

a

Tear off 1 square of TP. Place your index finger at the upper right corner. Roll the paper around your finger tip to form a tube.

b   *Twist here*

Twist the tube tightly, just below your finger tip, to form the flower bud.

c

Grasp the lower loose corner—point x.

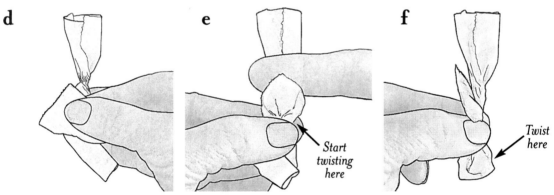

d

Pull point x up to the base of the flower, and shape it into a leaf.

e   *Start twisting here*

To form the stem, tightly twist all paper from the bottom of the leaf downward.

f   *Twist here*

When you are finished twisting the stem, pivot the leaf outward, and fluff it into shape.

7. Insert tweezers into the center of the rosebud, grab the loose corner, and twist it tighter to make a pretty center.

8. Cut a 3 ½-by-5 ½-inch piece of cardstock. Fold it in half widthwise to make a tent. Cut a 2-inch square of copy paper. Tape the copy paper to the cardstock, ⅜ inch from the left edge—and centered vertically. Inscribe with a guest's name. (Or use a computer to type your guest's name, and cut the copy paper afterward.)

9. Cut 2 parallel slits with a craft knife, each about ¾ inch long, ⅛ inch apart, and midway up the right side of the cardstock (see project illustration). Pull up on the strip, and insert the rosebud stem. Repeat to make as many place cards as needed.

Ruffled Heart Card

Red paper, ribbon, and ruffles are a classic combination for Valentine gifts and greetings. Inspired by heart-shaped candy boxes, this project is just as frilly, just as sweet—and filled with love. A heart-shaped pocket on the back can hold a photograph, a note, or a gift card to complete your present.

Supplies: 2-ply toilet paper, sewing machine, white thread, scissors, red cardstock (three 8 ½-by-11-inch sheets), white copy paper, craft knife, pen, yardstick, ribbon, white glue, double-stick tape, perfume (optional)

Instructions

1. Ruffle: Tear off a 15-square strip of toilet paper. Gather it along 1 lengthwise edge. To gather, machine stitch ¼ inch from the edge using a long stitch length, then stitch again, ¼ inch from the first stitchline. Pull on the bobbin threads, and push the toilet paper toward the center of the strip. Gather until the strip is about 20 inches long. Knot the threads at one end.

2. Using the template labeled Heart A, cut a heart from red cardstock . Squeeze a line of glue around the perimeter, ¼ inch from the edge. Starting with the knotted end of the ruffle, attach it at the top of the heart by aligning the 2nd stitchline with the edge of the heart. (Be sure the stitchline doesn't extend beyond the edge of the cardstock.) Continue sticking the ruffle to the glue line in this manner. Adjust the gathers to fit as you near the end. Cut away any excess toilet paper, and trim the threads.

3. Using the template labeled Heart A, cut another heart from red cardstock. Squeeze a line of glue around the ruffle—between stitchlines. Place the 2nd red heart so that the stitchlines will be covered. Press to attach.

4. Using the template labeled Heart B, cut a white heart from copy paper. Write a message, and attach it to the center of a red heart with double-stick tape. This will be the card front. (You could also print your message from a computer, and cut it into a heart afterward.)

5. Tie a piece of ribbon into a small bow. Glue it to the center front of the card where the ruffle meets the cardstock. Separate the toilet paper plies around the ruffle.

6. Pocket: Using the template labeled Heart B, cut a heart from red cardstock. Apply glue along the side edges, avoiding the top. Attach it to the lower back. Let the glue dry. Use the pocket to hold a note, money, a photograph, or a gift card.

TOP TIP
Spray the ruffle lightly with perfume

Copy-or-Trace
Template

HEART A

Copy-or-Trace
Template

HEART B

ANGEL SO SOFT

Give your home a heavenly touch for the holidays with a host of angels. A toilet paper tube provides the structure for this project, while simple punched holes make the skirt look like lace.

Supplies: toilet paper, toilet paper tube, sewing machine, white thread, hot glue, white glue, scissors, clothes pin, hole punch, pearlescent or metallic pipe cleaner, Scotch tape, Krylon silver glitter spray (optional)

Instructions

1. Body: Cut lengthwise across a toilet paper tube. Shape it into a cone, making the opening at the narrow end about ⅞ inch diameter. Hold the cone in place with a clothes pin, and secure it with hot glue. Remove the clothes pin after the glue sets. Trim the edges of the cone to be even.

2. Skirt: Tear off a 5-square strip of toilet paper. Fan-fold it on the perforations. Hold the Eyelet Edging template against one lengthwise edge, and punch holes. (Punch through all layers at the same time.) Unfold. Machine stitch—with a long stitch length—along the opposite edge from the holes. Pull on the bobbin threads while pushing the toilet paper toward the center of the strip. Adjust the gathered edge to fit around the top of the cone. Glue it in place with white glue. Trim the thread ends.

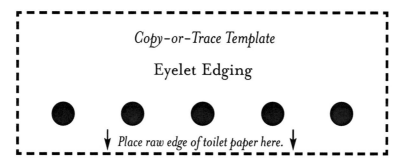

Copy-or-Trace Template

Eyelet Edging

↓ *Place raw edge of toilet paper here.* ↓

3. Collar: Tear off 1 square of toilet paper, and follow steps a-c.

a

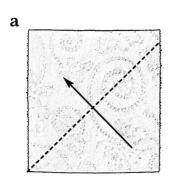

b

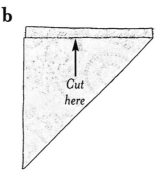

Cut here

c

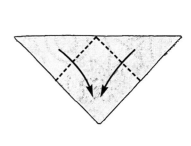

Fold the lower right corner up to the left edge.

Trim away the excess to make the top edges even.

Fold the right and left corners down to meet the lower point. The lower point is the bottom of the collar.

4. Position the collar at the top of the cone (refer to the project illustration on page 118). Fold the upper tip to the inside of the cone, and glue it in place.

5. Head: Tear off a 6-square strip of toilet paper. Crumple it into a ball by rolling it in your palms like a piece of dough. Tear off a 3-square strip of toilet paper, and place the ball at the center (**d**). Wrap the strip smoothly over the ball. Pinch the toilet paper together at the base of the ball, and secure it with Scotch tape (**e**). Insert the tail ends of the head piece into the top of the cone. Glue the head to the rim with white glue.

d

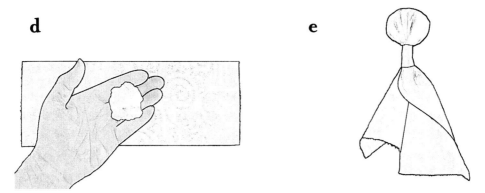

e

6. Halo: Wrap 1 end of a pipe cleaner around the angel's neck, and twist it at the center back to secure. Bend the tail end upward, and shape it into a loop over the head.

7. Wings: Tear off a 2-square strip of toilet paper and follow steps f-h.

f

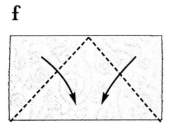

Fold the upper corners down to meet the lower edge.

g

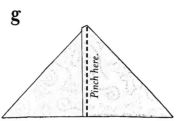

Pinch the paper along the center to shape the wings.

h

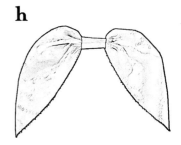

Wrap a piece of tape around the center to secure.

8. Final assembly: Tuck the wings in place between the pipe cleaner and the angel. Coat the angel lightly with glitter spray, if desired.

TOP TIP
Make your angel more ornate by punching holes in the collar and wings.

ORIGAMI HEART

For a speedy way to show some love, try your hand at origami hearts. Make them to decorate a Valentine's Day tablecloth, a bed pillow, a gift, a card, or just for fun! Kids of all ages will enjoy this one.

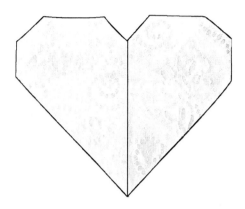

Supplies: toilet paper

Instructions

a

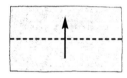

Tear off a 2-square strip of TP. Fold it in half lengthwise.

b

Fold both sides up along the center. Use the perforations for a guideline.

c

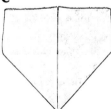

Flip the piece over horizontally.

d

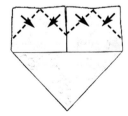

Fold the 4 upper corners down to meet at the center.

e

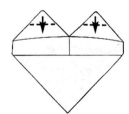

Fold each of the upper tips down— about ½ inch.

f

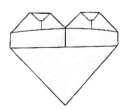

Flip the piece over . . . and you'll be finished.

Embossed Greeting Cards

Making an impression with toilet paper is easy and attractive. Using a technique that children and adults alike can enjoy, wet toilet tissue is pressed into a rubber stamp to create a cast image. There's plenty of room to express your creativity on the final product by adding color, punched holes, torn edges, or glitter spray.

Supplies: toilet paper, small glass plate, water, paper plate, soft cloth rag, rubber stamp, 8 ½-by-11-inch cardstock, double-stick tape, Krylon silver glitter spray (optional), non-aerosol travel hairspray and food coloring (optional), ink pad (optional)

Instructions

1. Fan-fold a 6-square strip of toilet tissue on the perforations. (Experiment with this quantity to see what you like best. Less layers can be better with detailed rubber stamps, while more layers will give your project more heft.) Lay the stack on a small glass plate, and cover it with water until it is soaked. Pour off the excess water. Dab a few times lightly with a dry cloth, pushing out any air bubbles.

2. Lift the paper carefully, and place it on top of a rubber stamp. Press all over with a cloth (microfiber is great), pushing the paper into the rubber stamp until you see a clear impression. Gently pull the toilet paper off of the rubber stamp, and place it on a paper plate.

3. Color: If you wish to color your embossing, add food coloring to hairspray, and spray on the wet toilet paper. For a beautiful effect, use several colors—spraying them in different quadrants of the toilet paper square—and overlapping them in some areas. *You can make multiple colors with one travel-sized bottle of hairspray by pouring out part of the contents, and coloring a portion at a time.*

4. Air dry, or dry in a microwave oven for 1 minute on medium-low. Check, and continue to microwave at 1- or 2-minute intervals until dry.

5. Use your piece as-is, cut it out, or tear around the perimeter for a ragged edge. To tear the edges—yet have them straight and neat—hold a ruler along the edge and rip along the ruler. At this point, I sometimes spray lightly with water to give the paper a more rippled, rustic effect—and dry it again. Decorate your piece further with punched holes or glitter spray, if desired.

6. Fold an 8 ½-by-11-inch piece of cardstock in half widthwise. Trim to a size that suits your embossing. Attach the toilet paper motif to the front of the card with double-stick tape. Inscribe the card with greetings.

TOP TIP

To give your embossing more definition, apply a light coat of ink to the rubber stamp before step 2.

LETTERS AND LACE BANNER

Make any occasion festive with lovely flags that come to life in the sunlight, and flutter in the slightest breeze. Add pizazz with colored letters to complement your decor, or mix it up and make each letter a different hue.

Supplies: toilet paper, small and large scissors, sisal twine or ribbon, glue stick, copy paper, computer and printer, decorative hole punches (optional)

Instructions

*This project uses a cutting method similar to making snowflakes.
Create a combination of hanging letters and lacy cutouts, or lacy flags alone.*

1. Flags: Tear off a 2-square strip of toilet paper. Fan-fold it lengthwise in 4 equal folds. You should have a narrow rectangle that measures about 1-by-8 inches.

2. Cutouts: Cut notches and curved shapes of various sizes into the side and bottom edges. Avoid cutting into the top inch of the rectangle, as this is where you will attach the flag to the twine. To get started, refer to page 126 for keys to various cut-outs and end treatments. Be creative with your cutting. Try fringes, or use decorative hole punches. A sharp, quality punch will cut through toilet paper. If you have difficulty, it is helpful to place a piece of copy paper under or over the toilet paper while punching. Keep in mind that when you are cutting on a fold, you are cutting half of a final shape. For example, to cut a heart, cut half of a heart into the fold. If you plan to add a letter to a flag, leave a 4-inch portion uncut in the center. Gently unfold the toilet paper when you are done cutting. Press the flag flat with your fingers, or iron it with a press cloth.

~

For occasions when words aren't necessary, lacy banners of cutouts are beautiful on their own.

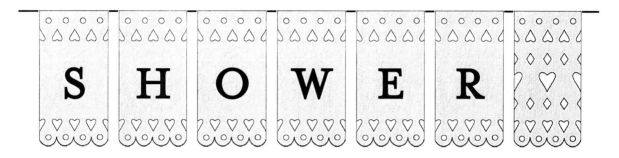

3. Letters: Print letters with a stylish font on your computer. Make them about 3 inches tall. Choose an ink color to complement your decor, or make each letter a different color. Cut the letters out. Leave a tiny border of white around each letter as you cut. It won't show against the toilet paper, and it is easier to show a neat edge. (If you don't have a computer, the letters can be cut from construction paper.) Apply glue stick to the back of a letter, and adhere it to a flag.

4. Repeat steps 1-3 to make as many flags as desired. Plan on a flag of plain cutouts (no letter) at each end of the banner and between words.

5. Assembly: Cut a piece of twine or ribbon that is long enough to accommodate your flags plus 4 extra feet. If your twine is too coiled, iron it. Leaving 2 feet of excess at each end, mount the flags on the twine. To mount, swipe a glue stick along the upper back edge of a flag. Fold the top over the twine, and press all layers together. Leave 1 inch of space between the flags.

TOP TIP
Don't get caught short!

Measure with twine across the area where you want to hang your banner. This will ensure that you have ample length.

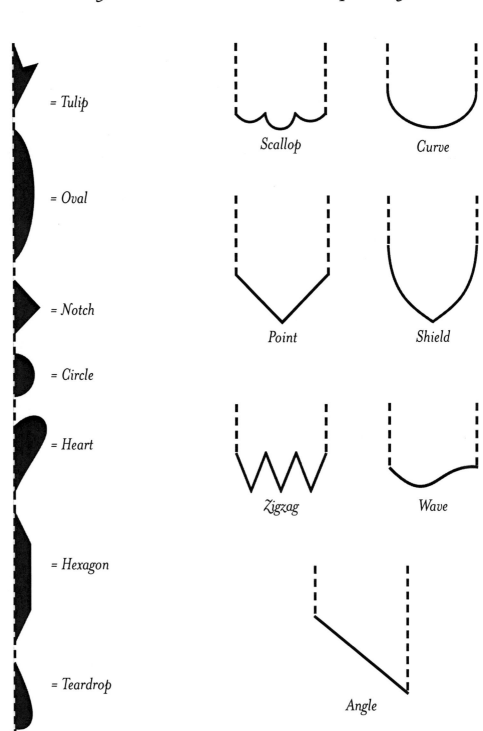

Cutout Key

= Tulip

= Oval

= Notch

= Circle

= Heart

= Hexagon

= Teardrop

Endpoint Key

Scallop

Curve

Point

Shield

Zigzag

Wave

Angle

Banner Inspirations

....

IT'S A BOY

JUST MARRIED

LOVE   HONOR   CHERISH

HAPPY ANNIVERSARY MOM & DAD

EAT DRINK & BE MARRIED

IT'S A GIRL

HAPPY BIRTHDAY

CONGRATULATIONS JAN & JOE

TIE THE KNOT

ANNA'S ROOM

HAPPY NEW YEAR

BEST WISHES

HAPPILY EVER AFTER

SWEET DREAMS

TOILET PAPER GAMES

Instructions

TOILET PAPER DRESS

A classic wedding shower game

Divide guests into 2 or more teams with at least 3 people per team. Each team chooses a bride, and are given rolls of toilet paper. Allow 20 minutes for each team to create a wedding dress on their bride using the toilet paper. When the time is up, the bride-to-be chooses the best wedding dress and gives prizes to the winners.

TOP TIP
Add extra prize categories such as the most original dress— or the funniest dress.

MUMMY WRAP

A party game for children

Divide party guests into teams of 2 or 3, and give them 2 rolls of toilet paper. Each team chooses 1 person to be their mummy. When the game starts, all teams race to see who can wrap their mummy in toilet paper the fastest—using all of the paper.

TOP TIP
Stock up on toilet paper and play this game a few times using different people as the mummy.

TOILET PAPER TALES

A getting-to-know-you game

Pass a roll of toilet paper to each participant and ask them to take as much as they like. Do not say any more about why they are taking the toilet paper or how much they should take. To play the game, each person must tell as many facts about themself as they have squares of toilet paper. For example, if someone has 7 squares, they must share 7 facts with the group. To help them get started, suggest examples such as where they live, how many children they have, where they were born, what they do for a living, what they do for a hobby, what kind of pet they have, their favorite color, etc.

TOP TIP
Give a prize to the person who took the most squares, or the least.

TOILET PAPER BELLY

A traditional baby shower game

Pass around a toilet paper roll, and ask each guest to tear off a strip that they think will match the circumference of the expectant mother's belly. When everyone has their strip, have them try it on the mother-to-be by wrapping it around the widest point of her tummy. The guest with the closest match wins the game.

TOP TIP
Have everyone put 1 quarter for every square of toilet paper on their strip into a piggy bank for the baby.

RESOURCES

The following toilet papers were my favorites at the time the designs in this book were developed, but be aware that bath tissue products change. Even as this book was being written, one of my favorites changed— in a way that was less suitable for crafting. Fortunately, there are plenty of choices on the market, and there were others to take its place. Future manufacturer modifications are bound to open up exciting new possibilities.

Page 9 DAHLIA, PEONIE & CARNATION: Full Circle or Bright Green. *Use a crisp 2-ply paper with plies that separate easily.*

Page 12 DAISY, COSMO, GARDENIA & POINSETTIA: Full Circle or Bright Green. *For the best results, use a crisp paper.*

Page 16 CHRYSANTHEMUM: Marcal.

Page 18 ROSE: Full Circle or Bright Green.

Page 20 BLOSSOMS & BIRDS MOBILE: Full Circle or Bright Green.

Page 24 POM POMS: Full Circle, Bright Green, or Marcal. *Choose a crisp 2-ply paper with plies that separate easily.*

Page 27 HONEYCOMB GARLAND: Cottonelle Ultra.

Page 28 PETAL MASKS: Cottonelle Ultra. Stick-It Felt is available at craft stores or joanne.com.

Page 38 PAPERWHITE WREATH: Full Circle or Bright Green.

Page 40 CONFETTI EGGS: Angel Soft Pretty Prints, Scott Soft Colors, Charmin Ultra Soft, or Cottonelle Ultra.

Page 44 GHASTLY GHOST: Full Circle or Bright Green.

Page 47 PARTY POPPER & SHAKERS: Full Circle or Bright Green.

Page 48 CUPCAKE TOPPERS & CAKE CORSAGES: Charmin Ultra Strong (Clown); Full Circle or Bright Green (Ruffle Flower and Lollipop Posy).

Page 54 FLOWER POWER: Marcal.

Page 56 DOGWOOD BRANCH: Full Circle or Bright Green.

Page 58 HOLIDAY GARLANDS: Cottonelle Ultra.

Page 62 EMBROIDERED TOILET PAPER: Charmin Basic. *This 1-ply paper will allow the embroidery pattern to show through.*

Page 68 TOILET PAPER CAKE: Angel Soft (cake) and Full Circle or Bright Green (flowers).

Page 70 ORIGAMI ROSE PARTY FAVOR: Charmin Basic.

Page 76 MUMMY COSTUMES: Cottonelle. Inexpensive garment blanks are available at www.dharmatrading.com.

Page 80 GIFT GARNISHES: Marcal (Giant Mum); Cottonelle Ultra (Kanzashi Flower, Money Roll, Here's My Heart, Pinwheel Bow, Starburst Bow, Florist Bow); Cottonelle (Classic Bow); Angel Soft (Rolled Rose); and Bright Green or Full Circle (Origami Butterfly).

Page 96 SNOWFLAKES: Cottonelle Ultra.

Page 98 TOILETREE: Full Circle or Bright Green.

Page 100 BUTTERFLY NAPKIN RING: Cottonelle Ultra.

Page 103 PAPER TRUFFLES: Full Circle or Bright Green.

Page 104 ROSETTE BROOCH: Charmin Ultra Soft.

Additional copies:

Give a copy of

TOILET PAPER CRAFTS
FOR HOLIDAYS AND SPECIAL OCCASIONS

for a gift.

For purchase information, go to

www.toiletpapercrafts.com

Also by Linda Wright:

TOILET PAPER ORIGAMI

Delight Your Guests with Fancy Folds
and Simple Surface Embellishments

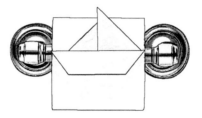

Learn easy yet eye-catching folds and embellishments
for styling the end of a toilet paper roll.

For purchase information, go to

www.tporigami.com

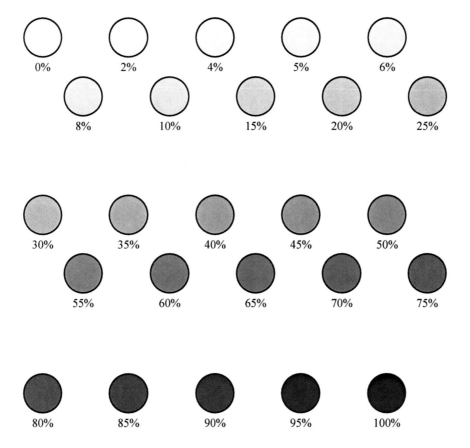

This dot gain chart has been inserted to help the publisher
monitor the printing quality of this book.

CPSIA information can be obtained at www.ICGtesting.com
Printed in the USA
LVOW112106110312

272569LV00003BA/21/P